Working with Sources

Exercises for
The Bedford Handbook
Ninth Edition

Diana Hacker

Nancy Sommers
Harvard University

Bedford / St. Martin's   Boston ◆ New York

Manufactured in the United States of America.

7   6   5

e   d   c

For information, write: Bedford / St. Martin's
75 Arlington Street, Boston, MA 02116
(617) 399-4000

ISBN: 978-1-4576-5057-4

A Note for Instructors

The exercises in this book offer practice in key research and documentation skills: forming research questions, determining effective thesis statements, integrating sources, avoiding plagiarism, recognizing common knowledge, documenting sources, and identifying citation elements in sources. If you have adopted *The Bedford Handbook* as a text, you are welcome to photocopy any or all of these exercises for a variety of possible uses:

- as homework
- as classroom practice
- as quizzes
- as individualized self-teaching assignments
- as support for a writing center or learning lab

This exercise booklet is also available for student purchase.

After a general exercise set on forming research questions, the exercises are organized by documentation style. If you ask your students to use MLA style, see exercises 53-1 through 56-8; for APA style, see exercises 58-1 through 61-8; and for *Chicago* style, see exercises 63-1 through 63-19. Most exercise sets begin with an example that is done for the student followed by five or ten items. Some items are multiple choice; others ask students to revise. The exercises are double-spaced so students can revise directly on the pages of the booklet.

This booklet includes a useful answer key (see pp. 139–53). Students will find correct answers accompanied by instructive feedback—so that they will never have to guess about why the correct answer is correct.

Contents

Chicago

EXERCISE 50-1 ◆ Research questions

To read about research questions, see 50b in *The Bedford Handbook*, Ninth Edition.

Circle the letter of the research question in each pair that would be appropriate for a college paper from ten to fifteen pages long. Remember that a research question should be focused (not too broad), intellectually challenging (not just factual), and grounded in evidence (not too speculative).

EXAMPLE

(a.) Why is the age of onset of puberty dropping among American girls?

b. Over the past two hundred years, how has the age of onset of puberty among American girls changed?

1. a. What is the current medical definition of schizophrenia?

   b. Which treatments for schizophrenia show the most promise?

2. a. What can be done to save our national parks from pollution?

   b. What can be done to combat air pollution at Grand Canyon National Park?

3. a. To what extent is solar energy an effective and economic alternative to fossil fuel energy?

   b. How many home owners across the United States use solar energy for part or all of their energy needs, and where do they live?

4. a. How have social media affected white-collar productivity in the American workplace?

   b. What impact are social media making on the business world?

5. a. How fair is affirmative action when used as a criterion for university admissions?

   b. When states have abandoned affirmative action as a criterion for university admissions, what have been the consequences to minority students and to the campuses at large?

6. a. What changes in social services were brought about by Jacob Riis's photographs of homeless and poor people in New York City at the end of the nineteenth century?

   b. What social services were available in New York City at the end of the nineteenth century?

7. a. What laws are needed to regulate the ways in which farmers cultivate and harvest their crops?

   b. Should the US government allow farmers to sell genetically engineered produce?

8. a. How can pharmaceutical companies be encouraged to provide low-cost drugs to combat AIDS in Africa?

   b. What drugs are desperately needed to combat AIDS in Africa?

9.   a.   What is morally wrong with allowing prayer—or at least a moment of silence—in public schools?

     b.   On what legal grounds has the Supreme Court refused to allow official prayer in public schools, and how has its decision affected elementary education?

10. a.   What are the provisions of Title IX, the 1972 act that banned gender discrimination in publicly funded US schools?

     b.   How has Title IX, which has banned gender discrimination in publicly funded US schools since 1972, affected college athletic programs?

Hacker/Sommers, *Working with Sources: Exercises for The Bedford Handbook*, 9th ed. (Boston: Bedford, 2014)

EXERCISE 53-1 ◆ Thesis statements in MLA papers

To read about thesis statements, see 53a in *The Bedford Handbook*, Ninth Edition.

Circle the letter of the sentence in each pair that would work well as the thesis statement for a research paper of about ten pages. Remember that a thesis should be a central idea that requires supporting evidence; it should be of adequate scope for a ten-page paper; and it should be sharply focused. Be prepared to explain your answer.

EXAMPLE

a. Although Thurgood Marshall and Martin Luther King, Jr., agreed that integration was a central goal of the civil rights movement, they did not see eye-to-eye on methods of achieving it.

b. Civil rights leaders Thurgood Marshall and Martin Luther King, Jr., were similar in many ways, but they had their differences too.

1. a. Residents of the District of Columbia must pay federal income taxes, even though they are denied voting representation in Congress.

b. Residents of the District of Columbia should be given voting representation in Congress because they pay federal income taxes.

2. a. When a woman suffering from postpartum psychosis does something terrible, such as injuring or killing her child, she obviously needs help.

b. When a woman suffering from postpartum psychosis injures or kills her child, she should be treated for mental illness rather than charged as a criminal.

3. a. Political and economic conditions in the early twentieth century help explain the popularity of Marcus Garvey's Back to Africa movement.

b. Marcus Garvey founded the Universal Negro Improvement Association and initiated the popular Back to Africa movement.

4. a. Because fighting terrorists who plan their activities online is a high priority for the US government, Congress should enact stricter computer privacy laws that allow for wiretapping and other forms of surveillance.

b. American citizens must give up their privacy rights so that the US government can find and convict political terrorists.

5. a. Online grocery shopping is gaining in popularity among American families.

b. Online grocery shopping benefits American families because it saves money, saves time, and lowers exposure to marketing gimmicks.

6. a. Seasonal affective disorder, common in northern countries such as Norway and Sweden, is a debilitating condition that affects many people during the winter months.

   b. Because light therapy and antidepressants do not always help those suffering from seasonal affective disorder, patients should also consider dietary changes and supplements.

7. a. Throughout history, big business interests have almost always been at odds with environmentally friendly practices.

   b. Although big businesses have traditionally been at odds with environmental interests, eco-friendly policies can actually lead to increased corporate profits.

8. a. There are both similarities and differences between the US AIDS epidemic in the 1980s and the Black Death that occurred hundreds of years ago in the Middle Ages.

   b. The US AIDS epidemic that began in the early 1980s had much in common with the Black Death of the Middle Ages: Both began mysteriously, terrified the general public, and seemed to some people to be God's punishment for sinful behavior.

9. a. The phrase "separation of church and state" does not appear in the US Constitution; Thomas Jefferson coined it in a famous letter explaining the First Amendment.

   b. Americans must continue to maintain the separation of church and state to protect religious minorities and to protect religion itself from domination by the state.

10. a. Wyatt Earp's law-and-order reputation is a myth based chiefly on a poorly documented biography written early in the twentieth century.

    b. Historians have shown that the reputations of many heroes of the Old West were based primarily on myths.

Hacker/Sommers, *Working with Sources: Exercises for The Bedford Handbook*, 9th ed. (Boston: Bedford, 2014)

EXERCISE 53-2 ◆ Thesis statements in MLA papers

To read about thesis statements, see 53a in *The Bedford Handbook*, Ninth Edition.

Circle the letter of the sentence in each pair that would work well as the thesis statement for a research paper of about ten pages. Remember that a thesis should be a central idea that requires supporting evidence; it should be of adequate scope for a ten-page paper; and it should be sharply focused. Be prepared to explain your answer.

EXAMPLE

a. The need for universal health care in the United States is more urgent than ever.

(b.) Universal health care would be an improvement over the current US health care system in terms of economics, access to care, and quality of care.

1. a. Legislators should not reinstate the Fairness Doctrine, which required broadcasters to provide balanced coverage of controversial topics; this federal policy had the negative effect of watering down political debate.

  b. The Fairness Doctrine, a federal policy that required broadcasters to provide balanced coverage of controversial topics, was abolished by the FCC in 1987.

2. a. The fascination with vampires among young people reflects our cultural obsession with immortality, youth, and individuality.

  b. What is it about vampires that attracts so many young people?

3. a. Many college professors spend too much of their time on publishing or research and too little time on teaching; as a result, they do a disservice to the students in their classrooms.

  b. Student evaluations of college professors should play a larger role in determining an instructor's overall performance and compensation.

4. a. More than one-third of the cumulative carbon dioxide emissions over the last century can be attributed to deforestation.

  b. Although much of the discussion about carbon dioxide emissions focuses on automobiles and factories, one of the most efficient ways of cutting emissions is through forest restoration and conservation.

5. a. While SAT scores are fairly accurate at predicting the academic success rates of white students, they are very poor at predicting the academic success rates of minority students.

  b. SAT scores should be eliminated from college admissions requirements because they do not accurately predict the academic success rates of minority students.

6. a. Although *Catch-22* is set during World War II, Joseph Heller uses the novel to comment on the absurdity of cold war society.

    b. Joseph Heller's novel *Catch-22* led to the widespread use of the term "catch-22," which refers to a paradox or a situation that cannot be escaped with a desirable outcome.

7. a. For roughly four decades, the war on drugs has attempted to make America drug-free, but this is an uphill battle with no end in sight.

    b. The war on drugs should be reformed to focus more on drug abuse education, prevention, and treatment rather than on law enforcement.

8. a. Public schools should consider the benefits of mandatory religious education, which can lead to increased tolerance of religious views.

    b. The teaching of religious education in public schools is a controversial topic, mostly because the First Amendment guarantee of freedom of religion has led to a separation of church and state.

9. a. Although the Civil Rights Act of 1964 guarantees workers the right to equal pay regardless of race, sex, religion, or ethnicity, more stringent laws are needed because the current law contains loopholes that allow unfair pay practices to continue.

    b. The Civil Rights Act of 1964 provided for the creation of the Equal Employment Opportunity Commission (EEOC), which, among other things, guarantees employees equal pay regardless of race, sex, religion, or ethnicity.

10. a. In 1884, nearly two decades after the Civil War and the abolition of slavery in the United States, Mark Twain wrote *The Adventures of Huckleberry Finn*; a century later, two decades after the passage of the Civil Rights Act, Toni Morrison wrote *Beloved*.

    b. Mark Twain's motivations for writing *The Adventures of Huckleberry Finn* were very different from Toni Morrison's motivations for writing *Beloved,* but both authors succeed in using their books to humanize the slave.

Hacker/Sommers, *Working with Sources: Exercises for The Bedford Handbook*, 9th ed. (Boston: Bedford, 2014)

EXERCISE 54-1 ◆ Avoiding plagiarism in MLA papers

To read about avoiding plagiarism, see 54 in *The Bedford Handbook,* Ninth Edition.

Read the following passage and the information about its source. Then decide whether each student sample is plagiarized or uses the source correctly. If the student sample is plagiarized, write "plagiarized"; if the sample is acceptable, write "OK."

ORIGINAL SOURCE

> The great and abiding fear of the South was of slave revolt. . . . For many Southerners it was psychologically impossible to see a black man bearing arms as anything but an incipient slave uprising complete with arson, murder, pillage, and rapine. The South was haunted throughout the war by a deep and horrible fear that the North would send—or was sending—agitators among their slaves to incite them to insurrection. That no such barbarous scheme was resorted to by the Union is a credit to the humanity and good sense of the Lincoln administration, although it was urged enough by some radicals.

> From Cornish, Dudley Taylor. *The Sable Arm: Black Troops in the Union Army, 1861-1865.* 1956. Lawrence: UP of Kansas, 1987. Print. [The source passage is from page 158.]

1. Civil War historian Dudley Taylor Cornish observes that many Southerners were so terrified of slave revolts that the sight of armed black men filled them with fear (158).

2. Many Southerners found it impossible to see a black man bearing arms as anything but an incipient slave uprising complete with arson, murder, pillage, and rapine.

3. Civil War historian Dudley Taylor Cornish asserts that "[f]or many Southerners it was psychologically impossible to see a black man bearing arms as anything but an incipient slave uprising complete with arson, murder, pillage, and rapine" (158).

4. During the Civil War, the Lincoln administration had the "humanity and good sense" not to send "agitators among [the] slaves to incite them to insurrection."

5. Although the Union ultimately sent black soldiers to the South, the Southerners' fears that the troops would incite a slave uprising were unfounded, in part because of the restraint of the Lincoln administration (Cornish 158).

Hacker/Sommers, *Working with Sources: Exercises for The Bedford Handbook,* 9th ed. (Boston: Bedford, 2014)

54-1 | Avoiding plagiarism in MLA papers   **7**

EXERCISE 54-2 ◆ Avoiding plagiarism in MLA papers

To read about avoiding plagiarism, see 54 in *The Bedford Handbook*, Ninth Edition.

Read the following passage and the information about its source. Then decide whether each student sample is plagiarized or uses the source correctly. If the student sample is plagiarized, write "plagiarized"; if the sample is acceptable, write "OK."

ORIGINAL SOURCE

Half of the force holding Fort Pillow were Negroes, former slaves now enrolled in the Union Army. Toward them Forrest's troops had the fierce, bitter animosity of men who had been educated to regard the colored race as inferior and who for the first time had encountered that race armed and fighting against white men. The sight enraged and perhaps terrified many of the Confederates and aroused in them the ugly spirit of a lynching mob.

From Castel, Albert. "The Fort Pillow Massacre: A Fresh Examination of the Evidence." *Civil War History* 4.1 (1958): 37-50. Print. [The source passage is from pages 46-47. The first sentence is on page 46. The rest is on page 47.]

1. Half of the force holding Fort Pillow were Negroes, former slaves now enrolled in the Union Army.

2. No doubt much of the brutality at Fort Pillow can be traced to racial attitudes. Albert Castel suggests that the sight of armed black men "enraged and perhaps terrified many of the Confederates and aroused in them the ugly spirit of a lynching mob" (47).

3. Albert Castel notes that 50% of the Union troops holding Fort Pillow were former slaves. Toward them Forrest's soldiers displayed the savage hatred of men who had been taught to view blacks as inferior and who for the first time had encountered them armed and fighting against white men (46-47).

4. Albert Castel suggests that much of the brutality at Fort Pillow can be traced to racial attitudes. Half of the Union troops at Fort Pillow were blacks, men whom the Confederates considered their inferiors. The shock and perhaps fear of facing blacks in battle may well have unleashed the fury that led to the massacre (46-47).

5. Why were the Confederates so brutal at Fort Pillow? Albert Castel offers an explanation: the sight of armed black men enraged and perhaps terrified many of the Confederates and aroused in them the ugly spirit of a lynching mob (47).

Hacker/Sommers, *Working with Sources: Exercises for The Bedford Handbook*, 9th ed. (Boston: Bedford, 2014)

EXERCISE 54-3 ◆ Avoiding plagiarism in MLA papers

To read about avoiding plagiarism, see 54 in *The Bedford Handbook*, Ninth Edition.

Read the following passage and the information about its source. Then decide whether each student sample is plagiarized or uses the source correctly. If the student sample is plagiarized, write "plagiarized"; if the sample is acceptable, write "OK."

ORIGINAL SOURCE

Apart from the fact that music accounts for much of the power of Hindi movies, creating a heightened mood that dialogue can rarely achieve, the film song spreads out from cinema to permeate many other areas of Indian society. Even before the advent of cheap audiocassettes, in the days when record players were rare and expensive, film songs achieved far-reaching popularity through street singers and wedding bands, which often played film hits rather than folk or traditional tunes. And the songs, with their inventive Hindi/Urdu lyrics (often written by celebrated poets), have long been a bonding force in the Indian diaspora, re-creating a familiar world of images and emotions and linking millions of people to their homeland.

From Kabir, Nasreen Munni. "Playback Time: A Brief History of Bollywood 'Film Songs.'" *Film Comment* May-June 2002: 41-43. Print. [The source passage is from page 41.]

1. In India, film music creates a heightened mood that accounts for a great deal of the power of Hindi movies, writes Nasreen Munni Kabir (41).

2. Nasreen Munni Kabir argues that the film songs disseminate from the movies to pervade several other aspects of Indian life (41).

3. Nasreen Munni Kabir notes that the songs in Hindi movies became widely popular even when few Indians owned recordings (41).

4. As Nasreen Munni Kabir explains, Hindi film songs managed to reach a broad audience "before the advent of cheap audiocassettes, in the days when record players were rare and expensive" (41).

5. Street singers and wedding performers helped film songs achieve a far-reaching popularity, according to Nasreen Munni Kabir (41).

6. Nasreen Munni Kabir points out that Hindi film songs not only contribute significantly to the effectiveness of the films in which they appear but also attract a worldwide audience of Indians who use them to reconnect to their roots and their communities (41).

7. In Hindi films, the songs have inventive Hindi/Urdu lyrics that are often written by celebrated poets.

8. According to Nasreen Munni Kabir, music in Hindi films pervades the culture both in India and abroad as it presents "a familiar world of images and emotions" (41).

9.   Hindi film songs have long re-created a familiar world of images and emotions to link millions of Indians to their homeland.

10.   Nasreen Munni Kabir believes that the beloved songs in Indian films have been "a bonding force in the Indian diaspora" (41).

Hacker/Sommers, *Working with Sources: Exercises for The Bedford Handbook*, 9th ed. (Boston: Bedford, 2014)

EXERCISE 54-4 ◆ Avoiding plagiarism in MLA papers

To read about avoiding plagiarism, see 54 in *The Bedford Handbook,* Ninth Edition.

Read the following passage and the information about its source. Then decide whether each student sample is plagiarized or uses the source correctly. If the student sample is plagiarized, write "plagiarized"; if the sample is acceptable, write "OK."

ORIGINAL SOURCE

Our four friends [in *The Wizard of Oz*] finally gain entry to the Wizard's palace because Dorothy's tears of frustration undam a quite alarming reservoir of liquid in the guard. His face is quickly sodden with tears, and, watching this extreme performance, you are struck by the sheer number of occasions on which people cry in this film. Besides Dorothy and the guard, there is the Cowardly Lion, who bawls when Dorothy bops him on the nose; the Tin Man, who almost rusts up again from weeping; and Dorothy again, while she is in the clutches of the Witch. It occurs to you that if the hydrophobic Witch could only have been closer at hand on one of these occasions the movie might have been much shorter.

From Rushdie, Salman. "Out of Kansas: *The Wizard of Oz.*" *Writers at the Movies: Twenty-Six Contemporary Authors Celebrate Twenty-Six Memorable Movies.* Ed. Jim Shepard. New York: Harper, 2000. 201-26. Print. [The source passage is from pages 223-24. Page 224 begins with the words *been closer at hand.*]

1. The sheer number of occasions on which people cry in *The Wizard of Oz* is astounding.

2. Rushdie notes that so many characters cry in *The Wizard of Oz* that it's surprising the Wicked Witch did not get wet and melt away earlier in the film (223-24).

3. Rushdie points out the number of characters who weep in *The Wizard of Oz*: Dorothy cries tears of frustration before being allowed to enter the Wizard's palace, the guard at the palace becomes sodden with tears, the Cowardly Lion cries when Dorothy hits him on the nose, the Tin Man nearly rusts up again from crying, and Dorothy cries again when captured by the Witch (223).

4. Pointing out how many times characters cry in *The Wizard of Oz*, Rushdie observes that "if the hydrophobic Witch could only have been closer at hand on one of these occasions the movie might have been much shorter" (223-24).

5. Rushdie notes that Dorothy's weeping makes other characters cry, as when her tears "undam a quite alarming reservoir of liquid" from the guard in an extreme performance outside the Wizard's palace (223).

EXERCISE 54-5 ◆ Avoiding plagiarism in MLA papers

To read about avoiding plagiarism, see 54 in *The Bedford Handbook,* Ninth Edition.

Read the following passage and the information about its source. Then decide whether each student sample is plagiarized or uses the source correctly. If the student sample is plagiarized, write "plagiarized"; if the sample is acceptable, write "OK."

ORIGINAL SOURCE

The conversations in the [James Fenimore] Cooper books have a curious sound in our modern ears. To believe that such talk really ever came out of people's mouths would be to believe that there was a time when time was of no value to a person who thought he had something to say; when it was the custom to spread a two-minute remark out to ten; when a man's mouth was a rolling-mill, and busied itself all day long in turning four-foot pigs of thought into thirty-foot bars of conversational railroad iron by attenuation; when subjects were seldom faithfully stuck to, but the talk wandered all around and arrived nowhere; when conversations consisted mainly of irrelevancies, with here and there a relevancy, a relevancy with an embarrassed look, as not being able to explain how it got there.

From Twain, Mark. "Fenimore Cooper's Literary Offenses." *Selected Shorter Writings of Mark Twain.* Ed. Walter Blair. Boston: Houghton, 1962. 227-38. Print. [The source passage is from page 236.]

1. Mark Twain notes that readers of James Fenimore Cooper are required "to believe that there was a time when time was of no value to a person who thought he had something to say" (236).

2. Mark Twain wonders if people ever conversed the way Cooper's characters do and if people really did have all the time in the world to listen to one another's ramblings (236).

3. Among Mark Twain's objections to Cooper's writing is the rambling conversational style of his characters, who seldom stick faithfully to their subjects but allow their talk to wander all around and end up nowhere (236).

4. James Fenimore Cooper's dialogue consists mainly of irrelevancies, with an occasional embarrassed-looking relevancy that can't explain how it got there.

5. Mark Twain ridicules the dialogue in Cooper's novels as sounding peculiar to modern ears; he points out that the conversations wandered all around and arrived nowhere (236).

Hacker/Sommers, *Working with Sources: Exercises for The Bedford Handbook,* 9th ed. (Boston: Bedford, 2014)

EXERCISE 54-6 ◆ Recognizing common knowledge in MLA papers

To read about what constitutes common knowledge in the humanities, see 54 in *The Bedford Handbook*, Ninth Edition.

Read each student passage and determine whether the student needs to cite the source of the information in an MLA paper. If the material does not need citation because it is common knowledge, write "common knowledge." If the material is not common knowledge and the student should cite the source, write "needs citation."

EXAMPLE

The playwright August Wilson won two Pulitzer Prizes in drama. *Common knowledge*
[Winners of well-known prizes such as the Pulitzer Prize are common knowledge because the information is readily available in any number of sources.]

1. Many of William Faulkner's novels are set in Yoknapatawpha County, a fictional part of Mississippi.

2. William Faulkner may have gotten the word *Yoknapatawpha* from a 1915 dictionary of the Choctaw language.

3. The writer and folklorist Zora Neale Hurston died in poverty in 1960.

4. William Shakespeare was the only playwright of his generation known to have a long-standing relationship with a single theater company.

5. Walt Disney fired and blacklisted all of his animators who went on strike in 1941.

6. William Wordsworth and Percy Bysshe Shelley were poets of the Romantic era.

7. As of 2012, the film *Titanic* had earned more than two billion dollars in box office revenue worldwide.

8. Heroic couplets are rhyming pairs of lines written in iambic pentameter.

9. Iris Murdoch wrote many sophisticated and complex novels before she succumbed to Alzheimer's disease.

10. George Lucas made a larger fortune by selling *Star Wars* toys than he made by selling tickets to *Star Wars*.

EXERCISE 55-1 ◆ Integrating sources in MLA papers

To read about integrating sources, see 55 in *The Bedford Handbook*, Ninth Edition.

Read the following passage and the information about its source. Then decide whether each student sample uses the source correctly. If the student has made an error in using the source, revise the sample to avoid the error. If the student has quoted correctly, write "OK."

ORIGINAL SOURCE

More than 1% of California's electricity comes from the wind. During breezy early mornings in summer, the contribution goes even higher. "At those times, the wind accounts for up to 8% of our electrical load," said Mary A. Ilyin, a wind researcher for Pacific Gas & Electric, the country's largest utility and a major booster of wind power.

Half of California's turbines . . . are located in Altamont Pass and feed directly into PG&E's grid. Most of the rest are found in two other major wind centers: Tehachapi Pass on the edge of the Mojave Desert between Bakersfield and Barstow, with a capacity of 458 megawatts, and San Gorgonio Pass north of Palm Springs (231 megawatts). Both are hooked up to the power lines of Southern California Edison.

From Golden, Frederic. "Electric Wind." *Los Angeles Times* 24 Dec. 1990: B1. Print.

1. Wind power accounts for more than 1% of California's electricity, reports Frederic Golden, and during breezy early mornings in summer, the contribution goes even higher (B1).

2. According to Frederic Golden, wind power accounts for more than 1% of California's electricity, and on breezy days "the contribution goes even higher" (B1).

3. Mary A. Ilyin reports that "wind energy accounts for as much as 8% of California's electricity" (qtd. in Golden B1).

4. On breezy summer mornings, says wind researcher Mary A. Ilyin, "the wind accounts for up to 8% of our [California's] electrical load" (qtd. in Golden B1).

5. California has pioneered the use of wind power. "Half of California's turbines . . . are located in Altamont Pass" (Golden B1).

Hacker/Sommers, *Working with Sources: Exercises for The Bedford Handbook*, 9th ed. (Boston: Bedford, 2014)

EXERCISE 55-2 ◆ Integrating sources in MLA papers

To read about integrating sources, see 55 in *The Bedford Handbook*, Ninth Edition.

Read the following passage and the information about its source. Then decide whether each student sample uses the source correctly. If the student has made an error in using the source, revise the sample to avoid the error. If the student has quoted correctly, write "OK."

ORIGINAL SOURCE

In 1827 two brothers from Switzerland named Giovanni and Pietro Del-Monico—the one a wine importer, the other a pastry chef—opened a shop on William Street [in New York City] with a half-dozen pine tables where customers could sample fine French pastries, coffee, chocolate, wine, and liquor. Three years later, the Delmonicos (as John and Peter now called themselves) opened a "Restaurant Français" next door that was among the first in town to let diners order from a menu of choices, at any time they pleased, and sit at their own cloth-covered tables. This was a sharp break from the fixed fare and simultaneous seatings at common hotel tables—so crowded (one guidebook warned) that your elbows were "pinned down to your sides like the wings of a trussed fowl." New Yorkers were a bit unsure about fancy foreign customs at first, and the earliest patrons tended to be resident European agents of export houses, who felt themselves marooned among a people with barbarous eating habits. The idea soon caught on, however; more restaurants appeared, and harried businessmen abandoned the ancient practice of going home for lunch.

From Burrows, Edwin G., and Mike Wallace. *Gotham: A History of New York City to 1898*. New York: Oxford UP. Print. [The source passage is from pages 436-37. Page 436 ends after the first dash in the first sentence.]

1. The Delmonico brothers' French restaurant was among the first eating establishments to let diners order from a menu of choices, at any time they pleased, and sit at their own cloth-covered tables (437).

2. As Edwin G. Burrows and Mike Wallace point out, restaurant culture in New York City changed forever with the arrival of the Delmonico brothers' French restaurant, which was among the first eating establishments "to let diners order from a menu of choices, at any time they pleased, and sit at their own cloth-covered tables" (437).

3. In their history of New York City's early years, Edwin G. Burrows and Mike Wallace describe the Delmonico brothers' first eating establishment, opened in 1827, as a shop consisting of "a half-dozen pine tables where customers could sample fine French pastries, coffee, chocolate, wine, and liquor" (437).

4. In 1830, the Delmonico brothers opened one of the first restaurants in New York City. "This was a sharp break from the fixed fare and simultaneous seatings at common hotel tables—so crowded (one guidebook warned) that your elbows were 'pinned down to your sides like the wings of a trussed fowl'" (Burrows and Wallace 437).

Hacker/Sommers, *Working with Sources: Exercises for The Bedford Handbook*, 9th ed. (Boston: Bedford, 2014)

55-2 | Integrating sources in MLA papers **15**

5. According to Burrows and Wallace, the Delmonico brothers' original shop enticed New Yorkers "with a half-dozen tables at which patrons could sample French pastries, coffee, chocolate, wine, and liquor" (437).

6. As Burrows and Wallace note, New Yorkers in 1830 felt "a bit unsure about [such] fancy foreign customs" as eating in a restaurant that offered a menu and separate tables (437).

7. Burrows and Wallace observe that the Delmonico brothers' restaurant first attracted resident European agents of export houses, who felt themselves marooned among a people with barbarous eating habits (437).

8. The Delmonico brothers' restaurant first attracted "resident European agents of export houses, who felt themselves marooned among a people with barbarous eating habits" (437).

9. According to Burrows and Wallace, "The idea [of a restaurant] soon caught on . . . and harried businessmen abandoned the ancient practice of going home for lunch" (437).

10. Native New Yorkers were at first suspicious of the concept of a restaurant. "The idea soon caught on, however; more restaurants appeared, and harried businessmen abandoned the ancient practice of going home for lunch" (437).

Hacker/Sommers, *Working with Sources: Exercises for*
The Bedford Handbook, 9th ed. (Boston: Bedford, 2014)

EXERCISE 55-3 ◆ Integrating sources in MLA papers

To read about integrating sources, see 55 in *The Bedford Handbook*, Ninth Edition.

Read the following passage and the information about its source. Then decide whether each student sample uses the source correctly. If the student has made an error in using the source, revise the sample to avoid the error. If the student has quoted correctly, write "OK."

ORIGINAL SOURCE

Most of us think that S.U.V.s are much safer than sports cars. If you asked the young parents of America whether they would rather strap their infant child in the back seat of the TrailBlazer [a Chevrolet SUV] or the passenger seat of the Boxster [a Porsche sports car], they would choose the TrailBlazer. We feel that way because in the TrailBlazer our chances of surviving a collision with a hypothetical tractor-trailer in the other lane are greater than they are in the Porsche. What we forget, though, is that in the TrailBlazer you're also much more likely to hit the tractor-trailer because you can't get out of the way in time. In the parlance of the automobile world, the TrailBlazer is better at "passive safety." The Boxster is better when it comes to "active safety," which is every bit as important.

From Gladwell, Malcolm. "Big and Bad." *New Yorker* 12 Jan. 2004: 28-33. Print. [The source passage is from page 31.]

1. Malcolm Gladwell points out that drivers feel safer in an SUV than in a sports car because they think that the SUV driver's "chances of surviving a collision with a hypothetical tractor-trailer in the other lane are greater" (31).

2. Gladwell argues that "active safety is every bit as important" as a vehicle's ability to withstand a collision (31).

3. A majority of drivers can, indeed, be wrong. "Most of us think that S.U.V.s are much safer than sports cars" (Gladwell 31).

4. According to Gladwell, American SUVs are more likely to be involved in collisions than other vehicles "because [they] can't get out of the way in time" (31).

5. Gladwell explains that most people expect an SUV "to survive a collision with a hypothetical tractor-trailer in the other lane" (31).

Hacker/Sommers, *Working with Sources: Exercises for
The Bedford Handbook*, 9th ed. (Boston: Bedford, 2014)

55-3 | Integrating sources in MLA papers **17**

EXERCISE 55-4 ◆ Integrating sources in MLA papers

To read about integrating sources, see 55 in *The Bedford Handbook*, Ninth Edition.

Read the following passage and the information about its source. Then decide whether each student sample uses the source correctly. If the student has made an error in using the source, revise the sample to avoid the error. If the student has quoted correctly, write "OK."

ORIGINAL SOURCE

With the liberalization in Africa of the rules governing used-clothing imports in the past ten years, Africans, who keep getting poorer, can now afford to wear better than rags. Many told me that without used clothes they would go naked, which, as one pointed out, is not in their traditional culture. And yet they know that something precious has been lost.

"These secondhand clothes are a problem," a young driver named Robert Ssebunya told me. "Ugandan culture will be dead in ten years, because we are all looking to these Western things. Ugandan culture is dying even now. It is dead. Dead and buried." The ocean of used clothes that now covers the continent plays its part in telling Africans that their own things are worthless, that Africans can do nothing for themselves.

From Packer, George. "How Susie Bayer's T-Shirt Ended Up on Yusuf Mama's Back." *The Best American Nonrequired Reading 2003*. Ed. Dave Eggers. Boston: Houghton, 2003. 224-36. Print. [The source passage is from pages 232-33. Page 233 begins with *Africans* in the first sentence.]

1. Packer notes "the liberalization in Africa of the rules governing used-clothing imports in the past ten years."

2. George Packer interviewed many Africans who feel that "something precious has been lost" with the arrival in Africa of cheap and plentiful used clothing (233).

3. One young Ugandan worries that the influx of Western clothing will devalue Ugandan culture, which he says is "dead. Dead and buried" (qtd. in Packer 233).

4. Packer asserts that Ugandan culture will not survive for another decade because Ugandans are becoming accustomed to Western goods (233).

5. An American reporter observes that the availability of Western clothing may send Africans the message that "their own things are worthless and they can do nothing for themselves" (Packer 233).

Hacker/Sommers, *Working with Sources: Exercises for The Bedford Handbook*, 9th ed. (Boston: Bedford, 2014)

EXERCISE 56-1 ◆ MLA documentation: in-text citations

To read about how to use and format MLA in-text citations, see 56a in *The Bedford Handbook*, Ninth Edition.

Circle the letter of the MLA in-text citation that is handled correctly.

EXAMPLE

The student is quoting from page 26 of the following source:

Hawley, Richard A. *Thinking about Drugs and Society: Responding to an Epidemic*. New York: Walker, 1988. Print.

(a.) "The use of cannabis has been traced back four thousand years to ancient China," writes Richard A. Hawley (26).

b. "The use of cannabis has been traced back four thousand years to ancient China," writes Richard A. Hawley (p. 26).

1. The student is quoting from page 26 of the following source:

   Hawley, Richard A. *Thinking about Drugs and Society: Responding to an Epidemic*. New York: Walker, 1988. Print.

   a. Richard A. Hawley reports that although the ancient Chinese used marijuana for medical purposes, "there is no record of the Chinese using it as a pleasure-producing drug" (26).

   b. Richard A. Hawley reports that although the ancient Chinese used marijuana for medical purposes, "there is no record of the Chinese using it as a pleasure-producing drug." (26)

2. The student is summarizing information from page 63 of the following source:

   Henningfield, Jack E., and Nancy Almand Ator. *Barbiturates: Sleeping Potion or Intoxicant?* New York: Chelsea, 1986. Print.

   a. Drugs classified as Schedule I by the Drug Enforcement Administration are illegal, even for medical purposes, but they are allowed in authorized experiments (Henningfield 63).

   b. Drugs classified as Schedule I by the Drug Enforcement Administration are illegal, even for medical purposes, but they are allowed in authorized experiments (Henningfield and Ator 63).

3. The student is citing a statistic that appeared in the following unsigned article:

   "Cross-Eyed and Painless." *Economist* 6 July 1991: 89. Print.

   a. Nearly half of 1,035 oncologists surveyed in 1991 said that if smokable marijuana were legal for cancer patients, they would prescribe it (*Economist* 89).

   b. Nearly half of 1,035 oncologists surveyed in 1991 said that if smokable marijuana were legal for cancer patients, they would prescribe it ("Cross-Eyed" 89).

Hacker/Sommers, *Working with Sources: Exercises for The Bedford Handbook*, 9th ed. (Boston: Bedford, 2014)

56-1 | MLA documentation: in-text citations **19**

4. The student is quoting from page 79 of the following source:

> Marshall, Eliot. *Legalization: A Debate.* New York: Chelsea, 1988. Print.

There are two works by Marshall in the list of works cited.

a. Marshall explains that marijuana can be dangerous for people with heart conditions because its use "can dramatically increase heart rate and blood pressure" (*Legalization* 79).

b. Marshall explains that marijuana can be dangerous for people with heart conditions because its use "can dramatically increase heart rate and blood pressure" (79).

5. The student is quoting from page 67 of the following source:

> Marshall, Eliot. *Legalization: A Debate.* New York: Chelsea, 1988. Print.

There are two works by Marshall in the list of works cited.

a. The US Drug Enforcement Administration has allowed marijuana to be used in experiments with patients suffering from glaucoma. According to one expert, "Several studies since 1971 have shown that smoking marijuana causes the pressure within the eye to decrease and to remain at a lowered level for about five hours" (*Legalization* 67).

b. The US Drug Enforcement Administration has allowed marijuana to be used in experiments with patients suffering from glaucoma. According to one expert, "Several studies since 1971 have shown that smoking marijuana causes the pressure within the eye to decrease and to remain at a lowered level for about five hours" (Marshall, *Legalization* 67).

6. The student is citing a statistic from the following short work from a Web site:

> United States. Dept. of Justice. Drug Enforcement Administration. "Drug Intelligence Brief: Mexican Marijuana in the United States, September 1999." *US Drug Enforcement Administration.* DEA, 10 Oct. 2001. Web. 3 Mar. 2005.

a. The Drug Enforcement Administration of the US Department of Justice reports that marijuana use among young people aged twelve to seventeen in the United States nearly doubled in the 1990s from 4.3% to 8.3%.

b. The Drug Enforcement Administration of the US Department of Justice reports that marijuana use among young people aged twelve to seventeen in the United States nearly doubled in the 1990s from 4.3% to 8.3% (n. pag.).

7. The student is citing a statistic from the following short work from a Web site:

> United States. Dept. of Justice. Drug Enforcement Administration. "1990-1994." *US Drug Enforcement Administration.* DEA, 12 Oct. 2001. Web. 5 Mar. 2005.

a. According to a report by the United States Justice Department's Drug Enforcement Administration, marijuana in the 1990s was about five times more potent than the marijuana of the 1960s.

b. According to a government report, marijuana in the 1990s was about five times more potent than the marijuana of the 1960s (Drug Enforcement Administration).

8. The student is quoting Rabbi Isaac P. Fried from page 38 of the following newspaper article:

> Treaster, Joseph B. "Healing Herb or Narcotic? Marijuana as Medication." *New York Times* 14 Nov. 1993: 38+. Print.

a. "I consider this [alleviating acute pain and nausea] a need that has to be filled," says Rabbi Isaac P. Fried of New York of his administration of marijuana to suffering patients. "Should I buckle under the fear of an archaic law that doesn't deal with the present needs of the 1990's?" (qtd. in Treaster 38).

b. "I consider this [alleviating acute pain and nausea] a need that has to be filled," says Rabbi Isaac P. Fried of New York of his administration of marijuana to suffering patients. "Should I buckle under the fear of an archaic law that doesn't deal with the present needs of the 1990's?" (Treaster 38).

9. The student is quoting from page 8 of the following article:

> Hecht, Brian. "Out of Joint: The Case for Medicinal Marijuana." *New Republic* 15 July 1991: 7-9. Print.

a. Brian Hecht sums up the debate over the medical use of marijuana in three questions: "(1) Is the drug safe? (2) Does it work? and (3) How does it compare with other available drugs" (8)?

b. Brian Hecht sums up the debate over the medical use of marijuana in three questions: "(1) Is the drug safe? (2) Does it work? and (3) How does it compare with other available drugs?" (8).

10. The student is summarizing part of the following article, written by six authors, from an online scholarly journal:

> Campbell, Fiona A., et al. "Are Cannabinoids an Effective and Safe Treatment Option in the Management of Pain? A Qualitative Systematic Review." *BMJ* 323.7303 (2001): n. pag. Web. 6 Mar. 2005.

a. Fiona A. Campbell et al. present the results of scientific studies on the effectiveness and safety of using marijuana for medical purposes.

b. Fiona A. Campbell presents the results of scientific studies on the effectiveness and safety of using marijuana for medical purposes.

Hacker/Sommers, *Working with Sources: Exercises for*
The Bedford Handbook, 9th ed. (Boston: Bedford, 2014)

56-1 | MLA documentation: in-text citations   **21**

EXERCISE 56-2 ◆ MLA documentation: in-text citations

To read about how to use and format MLA in-text citations, see 56a in *The Bedford Handbook*, Ninth Edition.

Circle the letter of the MLA in-text citation that is handled correctly.

EXAMPLE

The student is quoting from page 163 of the following book:

> Hentoff, Nat. *Listen to the Stories.* New York: Harper, 1995. Print.

(a.) An interviewer explains that country musician Merle Haggard "is not happy about much that is currently being packaged as 'country.' He will name no names but is manifestly disgusted by most of what's on the charts" (Hentoff 163).

b. An interviewer explains that country musician Merle Haggard "is not happy about much that is currently being packaged as 'country.' He will name no names but is manifestly disgusted by most of what's on the charts" (163).

1. The student is quoting from page 148 of the following magazine article:

   > Als, Hilton. "Wayward Girl." *New Yorker* 18-25 Aug. 2003: 147-49. Print.

   a. Als describes Cat Power as "a storyteller . . . [who] cares more about how she says something than about what she says." (148)

   b. Als describes Cat Power as "a storyteller . . . [who] cares more about how she says something than about what she says" (148).

2. The student is quoting from page 420 of the following book:

   > Kerman, Joseph, and Gary Tomlinson. *Listen.* 6th ed. Boston: Bedford, 2008. Print.

   a. Kerman and Tomlinson assert that punk rockers "reacted against the commercial flashiness of much rock with what we might call an anti-aesthetic: All expression was possible, including no expression. All musical expertise was acceptable, including none" (420).

   b. Kerman asserts that punk rockers "reacted against the commercial flashiness of much rock with what we might call an anti-aesthetic: All expression was possible, including no expression. All musical expertise was acceptable, including none" (420).

3. The student is summarizing two magazine articles:

   > Gates, David. "Report from a City of Ruins." Rev. of *The Rising,* by Bruce Springsteen. *Newsweek* 29 July 2002: 56. Print.

   > Santoro, Gene. "Hey, He's Bruce." *Nation* 16 Sept. 2002: 32-34. Print.

   a. In his album *The Rising,* Bruce Springsteen elevates his typical working-class subjects to the status of heroes in the post–September 11 world (Gates; Santoro).

   b. In his album *The Rising,* Bruce Springsteen elevates his typical working-class subjects to the status of heroes in the post–September 11 world (Gates, Santoro).

Hacker/Sommers, *Working with Sources: Exercises for
The Bedford Handbook,* 9th ed. (Boston: Bedford, 2014)

56-2 | MLA documentation: in-text citations   **23**

4. The student is quoting from page 281 of the following article in an anthology:

> Mead, Rebecca. "Sex, Drugs, and Fiddling." *Da Capo Best Music Writing 2000*. Ed. Peter Guralnick and Douglas Wolk. Cambridge: Da Capo, 2000. 281-93. Print.

    a. One startling description of fiddler Ashley MacIsaac begins, "Although wrecking a hotel room is standard rock-star behavior, it is unusual for the instrument of destruction to be a bucketful of freshly cooked lobsters" (Mead 281).

    b. One startling description of fiddler Ashley MacIsaac begins, "Although wrecking a hotel room is standard rock-star behavior, it is unusual for the instrument of destruction to be a bucketful of freshly cooked lobsters" (Guralnick and Wolk 281).

5. The student is quoting from page 623 of the following essay in an anthology:

> Bangs, Lester. "Where Were You When Elvis Died?" *Rock and Roll Is Here to Stay*. Ed. William McKeen. New York: Norton, 2000. 623-27. Print.

The paper includes another work by Bangs.

    a. Bangs argues that he sees Elvis Presley not "as a tragic figure . . . [but] more like the Pentagon, a giant armored institution nobody knows anything about except that its power is legendary" (623).

    b. Bangs argues that he sees Elvis Presley not "as a tragic figure . . . [but] more like the Pentagon, a giant armored institution nobody knows anything about except that its power is legendary" ("Where Were You" 623).

6. The student is quoting from page 136 of the following essay:

> Orlean, Susan. "Meet the Shaggs." *Da Capo Best Music Writing 2000*. Ed. Peter Guralnick and Douglas Wolk. Cambridge: Da Capo, 2000. 134-46. Print.

    a. The Wiggin sisters grew up in Fremont, New Hampshire. A town historian once wrote about Fremont that "for the most part, death, sickness, disease, accidents, bad weather, loneliness, strenuous hard work, insect-infested foods, prowling predatory animals, and countless inconveniences marked day-to-day existence" (Orlean 136).

    b. The Wiggin sisters grew up in Fremont, New Hampshire. A town historian once wrote about Fremont that "for the most part, death, sickness, disease, accidents, bad weather, loneliness, strenuous hard work, insect-infested foods, prowling predatory animals, and countless inconveniences marked day-to-day existence" (qtd. in Orlean 136).

7. The student is quoting from page E5 of the following newspaper article:

> Ratliff, Ben. "A Hall with Jazz on Its Mind; Basing a Season on Performers and New Works." *New York Times* 12 May 2004: E1+. Print.

    a. Ratliff notes that Lincoln Center's jazz concerts have been held at Alice Tully Hall and Avery Fisher Hall, "respectable cultural landmarks that are nevertheless physically hostile to the sound of jazz percussion" (E5).

24   **56-2** | MLA documentation: in-text citations

Hacker/Sommers, *Working with Sources: Exercises for The Bedford Handbook*, 9th ed. (Boston: Bedford, 2014)

b. Ratliff notes that Lincoln Center's jazz concerts have been held at Alice Tully Hall and Avery Fisher Hall, "respectable cultural landmarks that are nevertheless physically hostile to the sound of jazz percussion" (E1+).

8. The student is quoting from the following online article:

> Wyman, Bill. "Joey Ramone, R.I.P." *Salon.com*. Salon Media Group, 15 Apr. 2001. Web. 6 May 2009.

a. Wyman maintains that "if you were a rock-loving youth in America's . . . Sun Belt in the mid-1970s, the Ramones gave you your first taste of what a *sensation* was."

b. Wyman maintains that "if you were a rock-loving youth in America's . . . Sun Belt in the mid-1970s, the Ramones gave you your first taste of what a *sensation* was" ("Joey Ramone").

9. The student is quoting from page 12 of the following magazine article accessed through a database:

> "U2's Spiritual Journey Defies Categorizing." *Christian Century* 13 Feb. 2002: 12-13. *Expanded Academic ASAP*. Web. 7 May 2009.

a. While U2's music is infused with religious imagery and explicitly embraces Christian themes, the band's hard-living lifestyle makes "some pietistic Christians . . . question the band's beliefs" (*Christian Century* 12).

b. While U2's music is infused with religious imagery and explicitly embraces Christian themes, the band's hard-living lifestyle makes "some pietistic Christians . . . question the band's beliefs" ("U2's Spiritual Journey" 12).

10. The student is quoting and paraphrasing the following online wiki entry:

> "Riot Grrl." *Wikipedia*. Wikimedia Foundation, 2004. Web. 8 May 2009.

a. *Wikipedia* notes that the term *riot grrl* "became an almost meaningless media catchphrase" that was rarely used by artists themselves (Anonymous).

b. *Wikipedia* notes that the term *riot grrl* "became an almost meaningless media catchphrase" that was rarely used by artists themselves ("Riot Grrl").

Hacker/Sommers, *Working with Sources: Exercises for The Bedford Handbook*, 9th ed. (Boston: Bedford, 2014)

56-2 | MLA documentation: in-text citations **25**

EXERCISE 56-3 ◆ MLA documentation: in-text citations

To read about how to use and format MLA in-text citations, see 56a in *The Bedford Handbook*, Ninth Edition.

Circle the letter of the MLA in-text citation that is handled correctly.

EXAMPLE

The student is quoting from page 187 of the following essay:

Pérez-Torres, Rafael. "Between Presence and Absence: *Beloved*, Postmodernism, and
Blackness." *Tony Morrison's* Beloved: *A Casebook*. Ed. William L. Andrews and Nellie
Y. McKay. New York: Oxford UP, 1999. 179-201. Print.

a. Amy describes the scars on Sethe's back as a tree, which, as suggested by Rafael Pérez-Torres, transforms "the signs of slavery . . . into an image of fruition instead of oppression." (187)

b. Amy describes the scars on Sethe's back as a tree, which, as suggested by Rafael Pérez-Torres, transforms "the signs of slavery . . . into an image of fruition instead of oppression" (187).

1. The student is quoting from page 195 of the following essay:

   Pérez-Torres, Rafael. "Between Presence and Absence: *Beloved*, Postmodernism, and
   Blackness." *Tony Morrison's* Beloved: *A Casebook*. Ed. William L. Andrews and Nellie
   Y. McKay. New York: Oxford UP, 1999. 179-201. Print.

   a. According to Pérez-Torres, *Beloved* "offers a radical revisioning and recounting of history" (195).

   b. According to Pérez-Torres, *Beloved* "offers a radical revisioning and recounting of history" ("Between Presence and Absence" 195).

2. The student is quoting from page 183 of the following collection:

   Twain, Mark. *Adventures of Huckleberry Finn*. 1885. Ed. Gregg Camfield. Boston:
   Bedford, 2008. Print. Bedford Coll. Editions.

   a. As the novel progresses and he gets to know Jim better, Huck begins to understand that a black slave can experience emotions too. After observing Jim's mourning for the family he left behind, Huck says, "I do believe [Jim] cared just as much for his people as white folks does for their'n" (Twain 183).

   b. As the novel progresses and he gets to know Jim better, Huck begins to understand that a black slave can experience emotions too. After observing Jim's mourning for the family he left behind, Huck says, "I do believe [Jim] cared just as much for his people as white folks does for their'n" (Camfield 183).

3. The student is quoting from page 52 of the following book:

   Morrison, Toni. *Playing in the Dark: Whiteness and the Literary Imagination*. New York:
   Vintage, 1993. Print.

Hacker/Sommers, *Working with Sources: Exercises for
The Bedford Handbook*, 9th ed. (Boston: Bedford, 2014)

56-3 | MLA documentation: in-text citations   **27**

a. Morrison criticizes white authors for using black characters as mere props to expose their own characterizations:

> Africanism is the vehicle by which the American self knows itself as not enslaved, but free; not repulsive, but desirable; not helpless, but licensed and powerful; not history-less, but historical; not damned, but innocent; not a blind accident of evolution, but a progressive fulfillment of destiny. (52)

b. Morrison criticizes white authors for using black characters as mere props to expose their own characterizations:

> "Africanism is the vehicle by which the American self knows itself as not enslaved, but free; not repulsive, but desirable; not helpless, but licensed and powerful; not history-less, but historical; not damned, but innocent; not a blind accident of evolution, but a progressive fulfillment of destiny" (52).

4. The student is quoting from page 32 of the following book:

Morrison, Toni. *Beloved.* New York: Plume, 1988. Print.

The works cited list includes another work by Morrison.

a. Morrison deliberately alludes to Twain's book by sending Amy on a hunt for huckleberries when she first encounters Sethe in the woods (32).

b. Morrison deliberately alludes to Twain's book by sending Amy on a hunt for huckleberries when she first encounters Sethe in the woods (*Beloved* 32).

5. The student is quoting from page 339 of the following essay:

Mayer, Sylvia. "'You Like Huckleberries?' Toni Morrison's *Beloved* and Mark Twain's *Adventures of Huckleberry Finn.*" *The Black Columbiad: Defining Moments in African American Literature and Culture.* Ed. Werner Sollors and Maria Diedrich. Cambridge: Harvard UP, 1994. 339-46. Print. Harvard English Studies 19.

a. Mayer claims that Morrison uses the character of Amy "to explore . . . the conflict between 'freedom' and 'civilization' in a society deeply affected by slavery" (339).

b. Mayer claims that Morrison uses the character of Amy "to explore . . . the conflict between 'freedom' and 'civilization' in a society deeply affected by slavery" (Sollors and Diedrich 339).

6. The student is quoting from the following online source:

Railton, Stephen. "Imaging 'Slavery' in MT's Books." *Mark Twain in His Times.* Electronic Text Center, U of Virginia, 2007. Web. 6 Nov. 2008.

a. Railton suggests that, "even after slavery has been abolished, there remains the problem of understanding what it was like, what its legacy is, what it says about the nation's culture" ("Imaging").

b. Railton suggests that, "even after slavery has been abolished, there remains the problem of understanding what it was like, what its legacy is, what it says about the nation's culture."

Hacker/Sommers, *Working with Sources: Exercises for The Bedford Handbook,* 9th ed. (Boston: Bedford, 2014)

7. The student is quoting from page 207 of the following article:

> Amare, Nicole, and Alan Manning. "Twain's *Huckleberry Finn*." *Explicator* 62.4 (2004): 206-09. Print.

a. Some critics have asserted that Twain, like many authors of fiction, "relies heavily on names for satirical gain" (Amare and Manning 207).

b. Some critics have asserted that Twain, like many authors of fiction, "relies heavily on names for satirical gain" (Amare et al. 207).

8. The student is quoting from a book review accessed online:

> Atwood, Margaret. "Jaunted by Their Nightmares." Rev. of *Beloved*, by Toni Morrison. *New York Times.* New York Times, 13 Sept. 1987. Web. 14 Nov. 2008.

a. As the *New York Times* points out in its review, "Toni Morrison is careful not to make all the whites awful and all the blacks wonderful."

b. As Atwood points out in her review, "Toni Morrison is careful not to make all the whites awful and all the blacks wonderful."

9. The student is quoting Mark Twain from page 377 of the following article in a collection:

> Kaplan, Justin. "Born to Trouble: One Hundred Years of *Huckleberry Finn*." Adventures of Huckleberry Finn: *A Case Study in Critical Controversy.* Ed. Gerald Graff and James Phelan. 2nd ed. Boston: Bedford, 2004. 371-81. Print.

a. As Twain himself has said, *Huckleberry Finn* is a book in which "[a] sound heart and a deformed conscience come into collision and conscience suffers defeat" (qtd. in Kaplan 377).

b. As Twain himself has said, *Huckleberry Finn* is a book in which "[a] sound heart and a deformed conscience come into collision and conscience suffers defeat" (Kaplan 377).

10. The student is quoting from the following article accessed in an online database:

> Hamlin, Annemarie, and Constance Joyner. "Racism and Real Life: *The Adventures of Huckleberry Finn* in the Undergraduate Survey of American Literature." *Radical Teacher* 80 (2007): 12-18. *Academic OneFile*. Web. 13 Nov. 2008.

a. Some critics argue that "students of Huck Finn can begin to see the social construction of race and its impact on blacks and whites through the novel's narrator, especially when the narrative is placed alongside something more contemporary like Morrison's work" (Hamlin and Joyner).

b. Some critics argue that "students of Huck Finn can begin to see the social construction of race and its impact on blacks and whites through the novel's narrator, especially when the narrative is placed alongside something more contemporary like Morrison's work" (Hamlin).

Name _____ Section _____ Date _____

EXERCISE 56-4 ◆ MLA documentation: identifying elements of sources

To read about how to handle the elements of sources in MLA citations, see 56b in *The Bedford Handbook*, Ninth Edition.

Circle the letter of the correct answer for each question using information in the source provided.

SOURCE: A WEB SITE

1.   Whom would you list as the author of this Web site in a works cited entry?

   a.   Shakespeare

   b.   Harry Rusche

2.   In your paper, you quote from the internal page "Shakespeare and the Players: Introduction." The update date on the internal page is 2003; assume that your date of access was March 3, 2013. How would you cite that internal page of the site?

   a.   "Shakespeare and the Players: Introduction." *Shakespeare's World at Emory University.* 2003. Web. 3 Mar. 2013. <http://shakespeare.emory.edu/introduction.cfm>.

   b.   Rusche, Harry. "Shakespeare and the Players: Introduction." *Shakespeare's World at Emory University.* English Dept., Emory Coll., 2003. Web. 3 Mar. 2013.

SOURCE: AN ARTICLE ACCESSED THROUGH A DATABASE

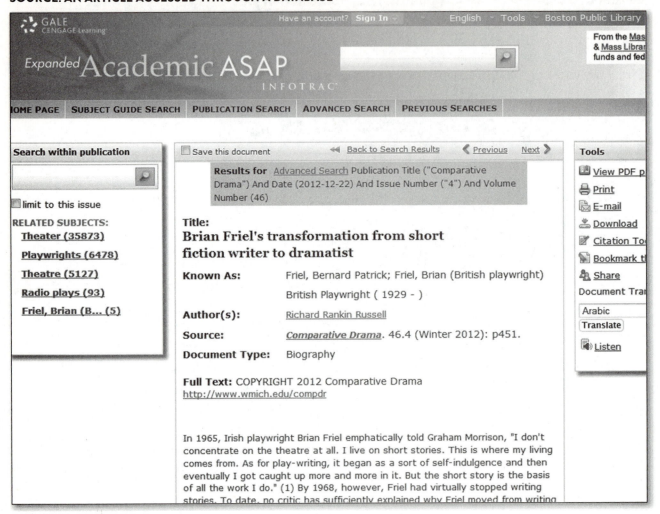

3. How would you cite the publication information for the journal article in this database record? (The article is more than one page long.)

    a. *Comparative Drama* 46.4 (Winter 2012): 451.

    b. *Comparative Drama* 46.4 (2012): 451+.

4. What information would you include after the page number in the works cited entry? (Assume that you accessed the article on March 29, 2013.)

    a. *Expanded Academic ASAP.* Web. 29 Mar. 2013.

    b. Web. 29 Mar. 2013.

Hacker/Sommers, *Working with Sources: Exercises for The Bedford Handbook,* 9th ed. (Boston: Bedford, 2014)

[Title page]

THE **SECRET LIFE**
OF **PRONOUNS**

WHAT OUR WORDS SAY ABOUT US

James W. Pennebaker

BLOOMSBURY PRESS
New York   Berlin   London   Sydney

[Copyright page]

Copyright © 2011 by James W. Pennebaker

All rights reserved. No part of this book may be used or reproduced in
any manner whatsoever without written permission from the publisher
except in the case of brief quotations embodied in critical articles or reviews.
For information address Bloomsbury Press, 175 Fifth Avenue, New York, NY 10010.

Published by Bloomsbury Press, New York

All papers used by Bloomsbury Press are natural, recyclable products
made from wood grown in well-managed forests. The manufacturing
processes conform to the environmental regulations of the country of origin.

LIBRARY OF CONGRESS CATALOGING-IN-PUBLICATION DATA

Pennebaker, James W.
The secret life of pronouns : what our words say about us /
James W. Pennebaker. —1st U.S. ed.
p.   cm.
Includes bibliographical references and index.
ISBN: 978-1-60819-480-3
1. English language—Pronoun.   2. English language—Grammar.   I. Title.
PE1261.P46 2011
425'.55—dc22
2011001289

Copyright © 2011 by James W. Pennebaker

All rights reserved. No part of this book may be used or reproduced in
any manner whatsoever without written permission from the publisher
except in the case of brief quotations embodied in critical articles or reviews.
For information address Bloomsbury Press, 175 Fifth Avenue, New York, NY 10010.

Published by Bloomsbury Press, New York

---

5. How would you begin the works cited entry for this book?

   a.   Pennebaker, James W. *THE SECRET LIFE OF PRONOUNS: WHAT OUR WORDS SAY ABOUT US.*

   b.   Pennebaker, James W. *The Secret Life of Pronouns: What Our Words Say about Us.*

6. How would you cite the place of publication for this book in an MLA works cited entry?

   a.   New York and Berlin:

   b.   New York:

7. How would you end the MLA works cited entry for this book?

   a.   Bloomsbury, 2011. Print.

   b.   Bloomsbury P, 2011.

SOURCE: AN ONLINE PODCAST

Slate Poetry Podcast, from *Slate*, copyright © 2011 by The Slate Group. www.slate.com. All rights reserved. Used by permission and protected by the copyright laws of the United States. The printing, copying, redistribution, or retransmission of the material without express written permission is prohibited.

8. How would you begin a works cited entry for the first podcast listed on this page?

    a. Ridge, Lola. "Manhattan." Narr. Robert Pinsky. *The* Slate *Poetry Podcast.*

    b. Pinsky, Robert, narr. "Manhattan." *The* Slate *Poetry Podcast.*

Hacker/Sommers, *Working with Sources: Exercises for The Bedford Handbook*, 9th ed. (Boston: Bedford, 2014)

[Title page of anthology]

The Consumer Society Reader

EDITED BY JULIET B. SCHOR AND
DOUGLAS B. HOLT

THE NEW PRESS
NEW YORK

[First page of essay]

5
Jean Baudrillard
"THE IDEOLOGICAL GENESIS OF NEEDS"[1]
(1969)

The rapturous satisfactions of consumption surround us, clinging to objects as if to the sensory residues of the previous day in the delirious excursion of a dream. As to the logic that regulates this strange discourse—surely it compares to what Freud uncovered in *The Interpretation of Dreams*? But we have scarcely advanced beyond the explanatory level of naive psychology and the medieval dreambook. We believe in "Consumption": we believe in a real subject, motivated by needs and confronted by real objects as sources of satisfaction. It is a thoroughly vulgar metaphysic. And contemporary psychology, sociology and economic science are all complicit in the fiasco. So the time has come to deconstruct all the assumptive notions involved—object, need, aspiration, *consumption* itself—for it would make as little sense to theorize the quotidian from surface evidence as to interpret the manifest discourse of a dream: it is rather the dream-work and the dream-processes that must be analyzed in order to recover the unconscious logic of a more profound discourse. And it is the workings and processes of an unconscious social logic that must be retrieved beneath the consecrated ideology of consumption.

1. CONSUMPTION AS A LOGIC OF SIGNIFICATIONS

The empirical "object," given in its contingency of form, color, material, function and discourse (or, if it is a cultural object, in its aesthetic finality) is a myth. How often it has been wished away! But the object is *nothing*. It is nothing but the different types of relations and significations that converge, contradict themselves, and twist around it, as such—the hidden logic that not only arranges this bundle of relations, but directs the manifest discourse that overlays and occludes it.

THE LOGICAL STATUS OF OBJECTS

Insofar as I make use of a refrigerator as a machine, it is not an object. It is a refrigerator. Talking about refrigerators or automobiles in terms

9. You have used the essay on the right from the anthology whose title page is on the left. What information would come first in your MLA works cited entry?

    a. Schor, Juliet B., and Douglas B. Holt

    b. Baudrillard, Jean

10. What information shown on these two pages do you *not* need in an MLA works cited entry for the essay?

    a. Edited by Juliet B. Schor and Douglas B. Holt

    b. 1969

EXERCISE 56-5 ◆ MLA documentation: works cited

To read about how to create and format an MLA works cited list, see 56b in *The Bedford Handbook*, Ninth Edition.

Circle the letter of the MLA works cited entry that is handled correctly.

EXAMPLE

The student has quoted from "Al Capone: Chicago," by Marilyn Bardsley, a short work on an unpaginated Web site, *The Crime Library*, sponsored by the Courtroom Television Network. The publication date is 2003, and the writer accessed the site on June 14, 2003.

a.   Bardsley, Marilyn. *The Crime Library.* Courtroom Television Network. Web. 14 June 2003.

(b.)   Bardsley, Marilyn. "Al Capone: Chicago." *The Crime Library.* Courtroom Television Network, 2003. Web. 14 June 2003.

1.   The student has quoted from "Al Capone," a short work on an unpaginated Web site, *The History Files*. The work has no author, and the site is sponsored by the Chicago Historical Society. The update date for this page is 1999; the student accessed it on October 9, 2002.

a.   "Al Capone." *The History Files.* Chicago Hist. Soc.,1999. Web. 9 Oct. 2002.

b.   Anonymous. "Al Capone." *The History Files.* Chicago Hist. Soc.,1999. Web. 9 Oct. 2002.

2.   The student has quoted from page 580 of *The American Promise: A History of the United States*, 5th edition, written by James L. Roark, Michael P. Johnson, Patricia Cline Cohen, Sarah Stage, and Susan M. Hartmann and published in 2012 by Bedford/St. Martin's in Boston.

a.   Roark, James L., et al. *The American Promise: A History of the United States.* 5th ed. Boston: Bedford, 2012. Print.

b.   Roark, James L. *The American Promise: A History of the United States.* 5th ed. Boston: Bedford, 2012. Print.

3.   The student has paraphrased page 163 of *Easy Riders, Raging Bulls*, a book by Peter Biskind that was published in New York in 1998 by Touchstone, an imprint of Simon & Schuster.

a.   Biskind, Peter. *Easy Riders, Raging Bulls.* New York: Touchstone-Simon, 1998. Print.

b.   Biskind, Peter. *Easy Riders, Raging Bulls.* New York: Touchstone, 1998. Print.

4.   The student has quoted dialogue from the 1972 film *The Godfather*, starring Marlon Brando and Al Pacino and directed by Francis Ford Coppola. The film was distributed by Paramount.

a.   Coppola, Francis Ford, dir. *The Godfather.* Perf. Marlon Brando and Al Pacino. Paramount, 1972. Film.

b.   *The Godfather.* Dir. Francis Ford Coppola. Perf. Marlon Brando and Al Pacino. Paramount, 1972. Film.

5.   The student has quoted from "Dapper Don's Time Gone," by Pete Hamill, published on June 18, 2001, on the news site *nydailynews.com*. The site is sponsored by Daily News, and the writer accessed the site on October 7, 2002.

a.   Hamill, Pete. "Dapper Don's Time Gone." *nydailynews.com.* Web. 7 Oct. 2002.

b. Hamill, Pete. "Dapper Don's Time Gone," *nydailynews.com*. Daily News, 18 June 2001. Web. 7 Oct. 2002.

6. The student has quoted Robert Towne from page 164 of *Easy Riders, Raging Bulls*, a book by Peter Biskind. The book was published in New York in 1998 by Touchstone, an imprint of Simon & Schuster.

    a. Biskind, Peter. *Easy Riders, Raging Bulls*. New York: Touchstone-Simon, 1998. Print.

    b. Towne, Robert. *Easy Riders, Raging Bulls*. New York: Touchstone-Simon, 1998. Print.

7. The student has summarized a review of *Gotham Unbound: How New York City Was Liberated from the Grip of Organized Crime*, a book by James B. Jacobs. The review, "Why Organized Crime Isn't What It Used to Be," by Albert Mobilio, appeared in the September 29, 1999, issue of the weekly newspaper the *Village Voice*. The writer accessed the article through the newspaper's Web site, *Village Voice*, on September 30, 2002. The site is sponsored by Village Voice.

    a. Mobilio, Albert. "Why Organized Crime Isn't What It Used to Be." Rev. of *Gotham Unbound: How New York City Was Liberated from the Grip of Organized Crime,* by James B. Jacobs. *Village Voice*. Village Voice, 29 Sept. 1999. Web. 30 Sept. 2002.

    b. Mobilio, Albert. "Why Organized Crime Isn't What It Used to Be." *Village Voice*. Village Voice, 29 Sept. 1999. Web. 30 Sept. 2002.

8. The student has quoted from "Sympathy for the (Jersey) Devil," an article by Joyce Millman published in the online magazine *Salon.com* on February 27, 2001. The magazine's site is sponsored by Salon Media Group. The date of access was October 1, 2002.

    a. Millman, Joyce. "Sympathy for the (Jersey) Devil." *Salon.com*. Salon Media Group, Feb. 27, 2001. Web. Oct. 1, 2002.

    b. Millman, Joyce. "Sympathy for the (Jersey) Devil." *Salon.com*. Salon Media Group, 27 Feb. 2001. Web. 1 Oct. 2002.

9. The student has quoted from page B1 of a *Wall Street Journal* article titled "Mobster Chic: It's Menswear a la 'Sopranos,'" written by Teri Agins and Joe Flint and published on March 10, 2003.

    a. Agins, Teri, and Joe Flint. *Wall Street Journal*. "Mobster Chic: It's Menswear a la 'Sopranos'" 10 Mar. 2003: B1. Print.

    b. Agins, Teri, and Joe Flint. "Mobster Chic: It's Menswear a la 'Sopranos.'" *Wall Street Journal* 10 Mar. 2003: B1. Print.

10. The student has quoted from an article titled "Violent Episode," published in *People* magazine on February 10, 2003. The article, for which no author is listed, appeared on page 126.

    a. "Violent Episode." *People* 10 Feb. 2003: 126. Print.

    b. Anonymous. "Violent Episode." *People* 10 Feb. 2003: 126. Print.

EXERCISE 56-6 ◆ MLA documentation: works cited

To read about how to create and format an MLA works cited list, see 56b in *The Bedford Handbook*, Ninth Edition.

Circle the letter of the MLA works cited entry that is handled correctly.

EXAMPLE

The student has quoted from a book, *India: A History*, by John Keay. It was published in New York in 2000 by Grove Press.

    a.   Keay, John. *India*. New York: Grove, 2000. Print.

    (b.) Keay, John. *India: A History*. New York: Grove, 2000. Print.

1.   The student has cited a book, *Cinema India: The Visual Culture of Hindi Film*, by Rachel Dwyer and Divia Patel. The book was published in New Delhi by Oxford University Press in 2002.

    a.   Dwyer, Rachel, and Divia Patel. *Cinema India: The Visual Culture of Hindi Film*. New Delhi: Oxford UP, 2002. Print.

    b.   Dwyer, Rachel, and Patel, Divia. *Cinema India: The Visual Culture of Hindi Film*. New Delhi: Oxford UP, 2002. Print.

2.   The student has cited an article, "Kishore Kumar," by Sushama Shelly. It appears on pages 95-96 of the November 2002 edition of the magazine *CinéBlitz*.

    a.   Shelly, Sushama. "Kishore Kumar." *CinéBlitz* Nov. 2002: 95-96. Print.

    b.   Shelly, Sushama. "Kishore Kumar." *CinéBlitz* November 2002: 95-96. Print.

3.   The student paraphrases material from an article, "Playback Time: A Brief History of Bollywood 'Film Songs,'" by Nasreen Munni Kabir. It appears on pages 41-43 of the May-June 2002 issue of the magazine *Film Comment*. The paper includes a citation of a book, *Bollywood: The Indian Cinema Story*, by the same author.

    a.   Kabir, Nasreen Munni. "Playback Time: A Brief History of Bollywood 'Film Songs.'" *Film Comment* May-June 2002: 41-43. Print.

    b.   ---. "Playback Time: A Brief History of Bollywood 'Film Songs.'" *Film Comment* May-June 2002: 41-43. Print.

4.   The student includes biographical information about Indian actor Rajkumar from an article titled "Rajkumar" in *Encyclopaedia of Indian Cinema*, which appears in a new revised edition edited by Ashish Rajadhyaksha and Paul Willemen. The encyclopedia was jointly published by the British Film Institute in London and Oxford University Press in New Delhi in 1999.

    a.   "Rajkumar." *Encyclopaedia of Indian Cinema*. Ed. Ashish Rajadhyaksha and Paul Willemen. New rev. ed. London: British Film Inst.; New Delhi: Oxford UP, 1999. Print.

    b.   "Rajkumar." *Encyclopaedia of Indian Cinema*. Ed. Ashish Rajadhyaksha and Paul Willemen. New rev. ed. 1999. Print.

5. The student quotes from a foreword by Aruna Vasudev in a book, *The Cinemas of India, 1896-2000*, by Yves Thoraval. The book was published in New Delhi in 2000 by Macmillan India. The foreword appears on pages vii-viii.

    a. Vasudev, Aruna. Foreword. *The Cinemas of India, 1896-2000.* By Yves Thoraval. New Delhi: Macmillan, 2000. vii-viii. Print.

    b. Thoraval, Yves. *The Cinemas of India, 1896-2000.* Foreword Aruna Vasudev. New Delhi: Macmillan, 2000. vii-viii. Print.

6. The student paraphrases material from an article, "Vijay Anand (1935-2004): A Belated Tribute," appearing on the Web site *Upperstall.com*, sponsored by Upperstall.com. No author is listed for the article, and the date of posting is 2004. The student accessed the site on May 12, 2004.

    a. "Vijay Anand (1935-2004): A Belated Tribute." *Upperstall.com.* 2004. 12 May 2004.

    b. "Vijay Anand (1935-2004): A Belated Tribute." *Upperstall.com.* Upperstall.com, 2004. Web. 12 May 2004.

7. The student summarizes material in a chapter titled "Hinduism" in the book *World Religions: A Historical Approach* by S. A. Nigosian. The student used the third edition of the book, which was published in Boston in 2000 by Bedford/St. Martin's. The chapter appears on pages 20-55.

    a. Nigosian, S. A. "Hinduism." *World Religions: A Historical Approach.* 3rd ed. Boston: Bedford, 2000. 20-55. Print.

    b. Nigosian, S. A. "Hinduism." *World Religions: A Historical Approach.* 3rd ed. Boston: Bedford, 2000. Print.

8. The student cites an article, "Bollywood Confidential," by Lisa Tsering. It appeared on the Web site *Salon.com* on January 28, 2003. The site is sponsored by Salon Media Group, and the writer accessed it on April 29, 2004.

    a. Tsering, Lisa. "Bollywood Confidential." *Salon.com.* Salon Media Group, 28 Jan. 2003. Web. 29 Apr. 2004.

    b. Tsering, Lisa. "Bollywood Confidential." *Salon.com.* 28 Jan. 2003. Salon Media Group, 29 Apr. 2004.

9. The student quotes dialogue from a film, *Lagaan*, directed by Ashutosh Gowariker and starring Aamir Khan and Gracy Singh. The film appeared on a DVD released in 2002 by Columbia TriStar.

    a. Gowariker, Ashutosh, dir. *Lagaan.* Perf. Aamir Khan and Gracy Singh. Columbia TriStar, 2002. DVD.

    b. *Lagaan.* Dir. Ashutosh Gowariker. Perf. Aamir Khan and Gracy Singh. Columbia TriStar, 2002. DVD.

Hacker/Sommers, *Working with Sources: Exercises for The Bedford Handbook*, 9th ed. (Boston: Bedford, 2014)

10. The student includes quotations from a review by Dave Kehr of the film *Lagaan*, directed by Ashutosh Gowariker. The review appeared on the *New York Times* Web site on May 8, 2002, under the title "The Cricketing of an Indian Village." The site is sponsored by the New York Times. The writer read the article on May 13, 2004.

    a.   Kehr, Dave. "The Cricketing of an Indian Village." Rev. of *Lagaan,* dir. Ashutosh Gowariker. *New York Times.* New York Times, 8 May 2002. Web. 13 May 2004.

    b.   Kehr, Dave. "The Cricketing of an Indian Village." *New York Times.* New York Times, 8 May 2002. Web. 13 May 2004.

Hacker/Sommers, *Working with Sources: Exercises for*
The Bedford Handbook, 9th ed. (Boston: Bedford, 2014)

56-6 | MLA documentation: works cited   **41**

EXERCISE 56-7 ◆ MLA documentation: works cited

To read about how to create and format an MLA works cited list, see 56b in *The Bedford Handbook*, Ninth Edition.

Circle the letter of the MLA works cited entry that is handled correctly.

EXAMPLE

The student has paraphrased information from the book *Breach of Faith: Hurricane Katrina and the Near Death of a Great American City*, by Jed Horne. The book was published in New York in 2008 by Random House.

a.   Horne, Jed. *Breach of Faith: Hurricane Katrina and the Near Death of a Great American City.* New
        York: Random, 2008.

(b.)   Horne, Jed. *Breach of Faith: Hurricane Katrina and the Near Death of a Great American City.* New
        York: Random, 2008. Print.

1.   The student has paraphrased information from a government report, *A Failure of Initiative*, written by the United States House of Representatives Select Bipartisan Committee to Investigate the Preparation for and Response to Hurricane Katrina. The report was published by the Government Printing Office in Washington, DC, in 2006.

   a.   Select Bipartisan Committee to Investigate the Preparation for and Response to Hurricane Katrina.
           A Failure of Initiative. Washington: GPO, 2006. Print.

   b.   United States. Cong. House. Select Bipartisan Committee to Investigate the Preparation for and
           Response to Hurricane Katrina. *A Failure of Initiative.* Washington: GPO, 2006. Print.

2.   The student has quoted from an article titled "The Katrina Conspiracies: The Problem of Trust in Rebuilding an American City," which was published in volume 35, issue 2, of *Journal of Urban History* in January 2009. The article appeared on pages 207-19 and was accessed on February 4, 2009, in the *Academic Search Premier* database. The authors of the article are Arnold R. Hirsch and Lee A. Levert.

   a.   Hirsch, Arnold R., and Lee A. Levert. "The Katrina Conspiracies: The Problem of Trust in Rebuilding
           an American City." *Journal of Urban History* 35.2 (2009): 207-19. Web. 4 Feb. 2009.

   b.   Hirsch, Arnold R., and Lee A. Levert. "The Katrina Conspiracies: The Problem of Trust in Rebuilding
           an American City." *Journal of Urban History* 35.2 (2009): 207-19. *Academic Search Premier.*
           Web. 4 Feb. 2009.

3.   The student has paraphrased information from an article titled "Hurricane Katrina as a Bureaucratic Nightmare." The article was written by Vicki Bier and appeared on pages 243-54 of the anthology *On Risk and Disaster: Lessons from Hurricane Katrina*. The anthology was edited by Ronald J. Daniels, Donald F. Kettl, and Howard Kunreuther and was published in Philadelphia in 2006 by the University of Pennsylvania Press.

   a.   Bier, Vicki. "Hurricane Katrina as a Bureaucratic Nightmare." *On Risk and Disaster: Lessons
           from Hurricane Katrina.* Ed. Ronald J. Daniels, Donald F. Kettl, and Howard Kunreuther.
           Philadelphia: U of Pennsylvania P, 2006. 243-54. Print.

Hacker/Sommers, *Working with Sources: Exercises for
The Bedford Handbook*, 9th ed. (Boston: Bedford, 2014)

56-7 | MLA documentation: works cited   **43**

b. Daniels, Ronald J., Donald F. Kettl, and Howard Kunreuther, eds. *On Risk and Disaster: Lessons from Hurricane Katrina.* Vicki Bier. "Hurricane Katrina as a Bureaucratic Nightmare." Philadelphia: U of Pennsylvania P, 2006. 243-54. Print.

4. The student has summarized information from two articles in the book *Hurricane Katrina: Response and Responsibilities,* edited by John Brown Childs and published in Santa Cruz, CA, by New Pacific Press in 2005. The first article is titled "The Battle for New Orleans"; it was written by Paul Ortiz and appears on pages 1-6. The second article is "Katrina and Social Justice" by Bettina Aptheker, and it appears on pages 48-56.

   a. Aptheker, Bettina. "Katrina and Social Justice." *Hurricane Katrina: Response and Responsibilities.* Ed. John Brown Childs. Santa Cruz: New Pacific, 2005. 48-56. Print.

   Ortiz, Paul. "The Battle for New Orleans." *Hurricane Katrina: Response and Responsibilities.* Ed. John Brown Childs. Santa Cruz: New Pacific, 2005. 1-6. Print.

   b. Aptheker, Bettina. "Katrina and Social Justice." Childs 48-56.

   Childs, John Brown, ed. *Hurricane Katrina: Response and Responsibilities.* Santa Cruz: New Pacific, 2005. Print.

   Ortiz, Paul. "The Battle for New Orleans." Childs 1-6.

5. The student has quoted from an entry in the work *Class in America: An Encyclopedia,* edited by Robert E. Weir and published by Greenwood Press in Westport, Connecticut, in 2007. The entry being cited is "Katrina" by Richard Jensen, and it appears on pages 415-18 of volume 2.

   a. Jensen, Richard. "Katrina." *Class in America: An Encyclopedia.* Ed. Robert E. Weir. Westport: Greenwood, 2007. Print.

   b. Jensen, Richard. "Katrina." *Class in America: An Encyclopedia.* Ed. Robert E. Weir. Vol. 2. Westport: Greenwood, 2007. 415-18. Print.

6. The student has quoted information from a segment of the program *Nightly News with Brian Williams,* which aired on MSNBC on August 29, 2006. The program was archived on *msnbc.com* and accessed by the student on February 21, 2009. The segment, reported (narrated) by Carl Quintanilla, is called "Katrina Money Spent and Wasted."

   a. "Katrina Money Spent and Wasted." Narr. Carl Quintanilla. *Nightly News with Brian Williams.* MSNBC, 29 Aug. 2006. *msnbc.com.* Web. 21 Feb. 2009.

   b. "Katrina Money Spent and Wasted." Narr. Carl Quintanilla. *Nightly News with Brian Williams.* MSNBC, 29 Aug. 2006. Web. 21 Feb. 2009.

7. The student has paraphrased information from a film on DVD titled *Inside Hurricane Katrina,* which was produced by the National Geographic Channel and released in 2006 by Warner Home Video.

   a. "Inside Hurricane Katrina." Prod. Natl. Geographic Channel. Warner Home Video, 2006. DVD.

   b. *Inside Hurricane Katrina.* Prod. Natl. Geographic Channel. Warner Home Video, 2006. DVD.

Hacker/Sommers, *Working with Sources: Exercises for The Bedford Handbook,* 9th ed. (Boston: Bedford, 2014)

8. The student has quoted information from a newspaper article accessed online on January 30, 2009. The name of the newspaper's Web site is *NOLA.com*, and the publisher is the Times-Picayune. The article was published on August 30, 2006, and is titled "Death. Loss. Rebirth." The authors are Bruce Nolan, Michelle Krupa, and Gordon Russell.

    a. Nolan, Bruce, Michelle Krupa, and Gordon Russell. "Death. Loss. Rebirth." *NOLA.com*. Times-Picayune, 30 Aug. 2006. Web. 30 Jan. 2009.

    b. Nolan, Bruce, Michelle Krupa, and Gordon Russell. "Death. Loss. Rebirth." *NOLA.com*, 30 Aug. 2006. Web. 30 Jan. 2009.

9. The student has paraphrased a blog entry titled "Katrina" written by Chris Matthew Sciabarra on his blog *Notablog*, for which a sponsor is not clear. The entry was posted on September 6, 2005, and accessed by the student on February 2, 2009.

    a. Sciabarra, Chris Matthew. "Katrina." *Notablog*. 6 Sept. 2005. Web. 2 Feb. 2009.

    b. Sciabarra, Chris Matthew. "Katrina." *Notablog*. N.p., 6 Sept. 2005. Web. 2 Feb. 2009.

10. The student has summarized information from an article on the Web titled "Post-Katrina Education Problems Linger." The article appears on the Web site *eSchool News* with the date August 30, 2007; the student accessed it on January 31, 2009. No author name is given, and eSchool News is listed as the sponsor of the site.

    a. eSchool News. "Post-Katrina Education Problems Linger." *eSchool News*. 30 Aug. 2007. Web. 29 Jan. 2009.

    b. "Post-Katrina Education Problems Linger." *eSchool News*. eSchool News, 30 Aug. 2007. Web. 29 Jan. 2009.

Hacker/Sommers, *Working with Sources: Exercises for The Bedford Handbook*, 9th ed. (Boston: Bedford, 2014)

56-7 | MLA documentation: works cited   **45**

EXERCISE 56-8 ◆ MLA documentation

To read about MLA documentation, see 56 and 57 in *The Bedford Handbook*, Ninth Edition.

Write "true" if the statement is true or "false" if it is false.

1. A parenthetical citation in the text of the paper must always include the following information if available: the author's name, the work's title, and a page number.

2. The works cited list is organized alphabetically by authors' last names (or by title for a work with no author).

3. The works cited list should include all of the works the writer consulted while researching the paper.

4. An in-text citation names the author (if there is an author) either in a signal phrase introducing the cited material or in parentheses after the cited material.

5. When a work's author is unknown, the work is listed under "Anonymous" in the list of works cited.

6. The list of works cited is titled Bibliography.

7. When a work has no page number, it is possible that nothing will appear in parentheses to mark the end of a citation.

8. In the parentheses marking the end of an in-text citation, use the abbreviation "p." or "pp." before the page number(s).

9. When a paper cites two or more works by the same author, the in-text citation includes at least the author's name and the title (or a short version of the title).

10. An entry for a Web source in the list of works cited gives the date the Web source was accessed.

Hacker/Sommers, *Working with Sources: Exercises for The Bedford Handbook*, 9th ed. (Boston: Bedford, 2014)

EXERCISE 58-1 ◆ Thesis statements in APA papers

To read about thesis statements, see 58a in *The Bedford Handbook*, Ninth Edition.

Circle the letter of the sentence in each pair that would work well as the thesis statement for a research paper from five to ten pages long. Remember that a thesis should be a central idea that requires supporting evidence; it should be of adequate scope for a five-to-ten-page paper; and it should be sharply focused.

EXAMPLE

(a.) Believers in so-called alien abductions think that extraterrestrials have contacted humans, but a better explanation for such experiences is the phenomenon known as sleep paralysis.

b. At least several hundred Americans—and perhaps many more—believe that they have been attacked in their beds by extraterrestrial beings.

1. a. American women who expect motherhood to be completely fulfilling will be seriously disappointed when they encounter the many unpleasant realities of child care.

   b. Because American culture usually depicts mother-child relationships as unambiguously positive, women who feel ambivalent about the sacrifices of motherhood can suffer from a depressing sense of isolation.

2. a. Psychologists who use their specialized knowledge to help advertisers target children should be censured by the American Psychological Association.

   b. It is unethical for psychologists to help advertisers find ways to convince consumers to buy a product.

3. a. Research has demonstrated that showing an eyewitness sequential photographs of suspects rather than a lineup reduces mistaken identifications, but for a variety of reasons most police departments in the United States do not want to change their methods.

   b. Many people are jailed—and some are even executed—in the United States based solely on eyewitness testimony, which can sometimes be mistaken, but little has been done to correct the problem.

4. a. According to a 1998 survey, 80% of the most popular video games contain violent or aggressive content.

   b. Studies have not conclusively proved that violent video games cause aggressive behavior, but new longitudinal research may lead to more conclusive results.

Hacker/Sommers, *Working with Sources: Exercises for The Bedford Handbook*, 9th ed. (Boston: Bedford, 2014)

58-1 | Thesis statements in APA papers **47**

5. a. Although adults often believe that children are emotionally resilient, a child whose brain is still developing is more likely than an adult to suffer long-lasting psychological damage from exposure to a traumatic event.

   b. People who suffer from post-traumatic stress disorder, or PTSD, may experience intrusive recollections of the traumatic event, feel less emotionally responsive than before the event occurred, and feel increased anxiety, irritability, and anger.

6. a. Many men and women have become so obsessed with body image that they are willing to turn to drugs, fad diets, and even surgery to achieve their goals.

   b. Rising rates of eating disorders among young women and girls in the United States are almost certainly linked to the pervasiveness of images of very thin models and actresses in American popular culture.

7. a. Milestone Comics, which was launched in February 1993, issued more than 200 titles in the four years of its existence.

   b. The failure of Milestone Comics, which published comic books featuring black superheroes created and drawn by blacks, occurred because distributors believed that their white clientele would not buy comics about black characters who were not stereotypes.

8. a. Although spending time online may cause people to have less face-to-face contact with their family and friends, online communities can offer as much intellectual stimulation and emotional support as real-world social contact does.

   b. When people spend a lot of time on the Internet, they become less involved in the communities in their lives, but the many benefits of being online may well make up for the social drawbacks.

9. a. Designed to prevent drug use by students, the DARE program has had an unintended consequence: As children learn more about drugs from sources outside of school, they become skeptical of the lessons they have been taught.

   b. Programs to prevent drugs and violence in schools, such as DARE and "zero-tolerance" policies, may do more harm than good.

10. a. Gays and lesbians should not face discrimination in housing, employment, health benefits, financial benefits, or any other aspect of life.

    b. Because marriage entitles the partners to share insurance benefits and pay lower taxes, states that do not allow same-sex couples to marry are discriminating financially against gays and lesbians.

Hacker/Sommers, *Working with Sources: Exercises for The Bedford Handbook*, 9th ed. (Boston: Bedford, 2014)

EXERCISE 58-2 ◆ Thesis statements in APA papers

To read about thesis statements, see 58a in *The Bedford Handbook*, Ninth Edition.

Circle the letter of the sentence in each pair that would work well as the thesis statement for a research paper from five to ten pages long. Remember that a thesis should be a central idea that requires supporting evidence; it should be of adequate scope for a five-to-ten-page paper; and it should be sharply focused.

EXAMPLE

(a.) Early-childhood intervention programs that focus on social and emotional development of disadvantaged youth deserve more funding because they have led to reductions in criminal behavior.

b. Early-childhood intervention programs for disadvantaged youth are very important.

1. a. More than one million school-aged children in the United States are educated primarily at home.

   b. Homeschooling is effective only when the correct social, emotional, and educational circumstances exist for both parent and child.

2. a. One way to ensure the early detection, effective treatment, and ultimate reduction of childhood mental health problems is to professionalize the child care industry.

   b. If we as a society don't do something to meet the mental health needs of very young children, we will all pay the price in the long run.

3. a. In 1997, the National Gambling Impact Study Commission found that the prevalence of pathological gambling was twice as likely to occur within 50 miles of a gambling facility.

   b. In Connecticut, where casino gambling and the state lottery contribute more than half a billion dollars a year to the state's revenue, more money should be spent on programs that can prevent and treat gambling addiction.

4. a. Although it has been criticized, the resource dilution model—the theory that the number of siblings a child has can influence his or her chances for intellectual development—offers the most likely explanation for why this causal relationship may exist.

   b. It is largely undisputed that children with no siblings are more likely to score higher on cognitive skills tests than children with multiple siblings.

5. a. Given the possible link between suicide rates and antidepressant medications in children and teenagers, physicians should more closely monitor first-time users of these drugs.

   b. Psychotherapy alone may be the right course of action for some depressed children, yet others may benefit more from a combination of therapy and medication.

6.   a.   Most American parents, aware of the reality of teenage sexual activity, favor comprehensive sex education programs rather than abstinence-only programs for their children.

     b.   Recent evidence suggests that abstinence-only sex education programs do not decrease the number of teenage pregnancies; in fact, these programs can actually increase the number of sexually transmitted diseases in teens because they do not incorporate a discussion of safe sex.

7.   a.   Although many people believe that the number of suicides increases during times of severe economic crises, there is very little evidence to support this theory.

     b.   Since the rate of suicides among Native American youths is more than twice the national average, federal agencies must make suicide prevention in our Native communities a top priority.

8.   a.   The pressure put on schools and educators for their students to perform well on standardized tests has resulted in higher scores but has not increased students' long-term ability to achieve.

     b.   Proponents of the federal No Child Left Behind Act (NCLB) point to its emphasis on teacher accountability, its focus on quality education for all children, and its provision for school choice; but critics charge that NCLB is underfunded, narrowly focuses on three subject areas, and ultimately has lowered overall education standards.

9.   a.   Merit-based pay schemes base teacher salaries on performance, as most private-sector companies do, rather than on seniority, as most public school districts do.

     b.   As can be seen in the success of many charter schools, merit-based pay schemes for teachers are one way to bring about improved student performance.

10.   a.   Considering the enormous debt this country owes to its military personnel and their families, the government should support programs that help reduce domestic violence in military homes, where rates of child abuse and spousal abuse are above the national average.

     b.   Domestic violence and substance abuse are much more prevalent in military families than in civilian families, especially during times of war.

Hacker/Sommers, *Working with Sources: Exercises for The Bedford Handbook*, 9th ed. (Boston: Bedford, 2014)

EXERCISE 59-1 ◆ Avoiding plagiarism in APA papers

To read about avoiding plagiarism, see 59 in *The Bedford Handbook*, Ninth Edition.

Read the following passage and the information about its source. Then decide whether each student sample is plagiarized or uses the source correctly. If the student sample is plagiarized, write "plagiarized"; if the sample is acceptable, write "OK."

ORIGINAL SOURCE

In everyday situations, behavior is determined by the combination of internal knowledge and external information and constraints. People routinely capitalize on this fact. They can minimize the amount of material they must learn or the completeness, precision, accuracy, or depth of the learning. People can deliberately organize the environment to support their behavior. Some people with brain damage can function so well that even their co-workers may not be aware of their handicap. Nonreaders have been known to fool others, even in situations where their job presumably requires reading skills. They know what is expected of them, follow the behavior of their co-workers, and set up situations so that they do not need to read or so that their co-workers do the reading for them.

From Norman, D. A. (1988). *The psychology of everyday things.* New York, NY: Basic Books. [The source passage is from page 55.]

1. According to Norman (1988), in everyday situations, behavior is determined by the combination of internal knowledge and external information and constraints (p. 55).

2. Norman (1988) has observed that "behavior is determined by the combination of internal knowledge and external information and constraints" (p. 55).

3. Norman (1988) has pointed out that people routinely minimize the amount of material they have to learn or they minimize the completeness, precision, accuracy, or depth of the learning (p. 55).

4. Norman (1988) has pointed out that people try to reduce the amount of work they have to do to learn new information. To expend less effort, they may learn as little as they need to do the task at hand or absorb information incompletely or imprecisely (p. 55).

5. "People can deliberately organize the environment to support their behavior," noted Norman (1988). "Some people with brain damage can function so well that even their co-workers may not be aware of their handicap" (p. 55).

6. At work, people can organize the environment to support the way they behave, according to Norman (1988). People with brain damage sometimes function so well that co-workers may not know of their handicap, and people who cannot read have been known to fool others even when their job apparently requires reading skills (p. 55).

7. According to Norman (1988), some workers who are brain-damaged or illiterate nevertheless manage to perform tasks well enough to keep their co-workers from knowing about their disabilities (p. 55).

Hacker/Sommers, *Working with Sources: Exercises for
The Bedford Handbook*, 9th ed. (Boston: Bedford, 2014)

59-1 | Avoiding plagiarism in APA papers **51**

8. Norman (1988) explained that some people who are brain-damaged or illiterate still manage to perform tasks well enough to keep their co-workers from knowing about their disabilities (p. 55).

9. Some people with brain damage can function so well that even their co-workers may not be aware of their handicap, and nonreaders have been known to fool others, even in situations where their job presumably requires reading skills (Norman, 1988, p. 55).

10. People who can't read have been known to dupe co-workers, noted Norman (1988), even when their job supposedly requires reading skills (p. 55).

Hacker/Sommers, *Working with Sources: Exercises for The Bedford Handbook*, 9th ed. (Boston: Bedford, 2014)

EXERCISE 59-2 ◆ Avoiding plagiarism in APA papers

To read about avoiding plagiarism, see 59 in *The Bedford Handbook*, Ninth Edition.

Read the following passage and the information about its source. Then decide whether each student sample is plagiarized or uses the source correctly. If the student sample is plagiarized, write "plagiarized"; if the sample is acceptable, write "OK."

ORIGINAL SOURCE

Mass psychogenic illness, or epidemic hysteria, is usually defined as a set of unexplained symptoms affecting two or more people; in most cases, victims share a theory of some sort about what is causing their distress. Often, somebody smells something funny, which may or may not be a chemical and which may or may not be there, but which in any case does not account for the subsequent symptoms. Relapses tend to happen when the people affected congregate again. And, notably, the mechanism of contagion is quite different from what you would expect in, say, a viral illness: symptoms spread by "line of sight," which is to say, people get sick as they see other people getting sick. Some element of unusual psychological stress is often at play. . . . Adolescents and preadolescents are particularly susceptible. And girls are more likely to fall ill than boys.

From Talbot, M. (2002, June 2). *Hysteria* hysteria. *The New York Times Magazine*,
    pp. 42-47, 58-59, 96, 98, 101-102. [The source passage is from pages 58-59. The
    word *Adolescents* begins page 59.]

1. Mass psychogenic illness, also known as epidemic hysteria, is a set of unexplained symptoms affecting two or more people who usually share a theory of some sort about what is causing their distress.

2. As Talbot (2002) has pointed out, victims of mass hysteria may believe that they have breathed in a strange odor that might or might not have been a toxic substance and that might or might not have been present; the chemical would not, in any case, explain the subsequent symptoms (p. 58).

3. In cases of mass hysteria, according to Talbot (2002), "Often, somebody smells something funny, which may or may not be a chemical and which may or may not be there, but which in any case does not account for the subsequent symptoms" (p. 58).

4. Talbot (2002) explained that people affected by an outbreak of epidemic hysteria usually "share a theory of some sort about what is causing their distress" (p. 58).

5. Talbot (2002) has described the peculiar nature of mass psychogenic illness, in which sufferers agree about the underlying cause—an odd smell, for example—of their physical symptoms and suffer relapses when they come in contact with other victims (p. 58).

6. People become ill when they see other people becoming ill, according to Talbot (2002), so the "mechanism of contagion" is not at all what you would expect in, for example, a viral ailment (p. 58).

7. According to Talbot (2002), epidemic hysteria differs in several ways from other contagious diseases; for example, relapses among victims tend to happen when the people affected congregate again (p. 58).

8. Talbot (2002) explained that mass psychogenic illness often afflicts people when they are under some kind of psychological pressure (p. 58).

9. Adolescents and preadolescents are particularly susceptible to mass hysteria, and girls are more likely to fall ill than boys are.

10. Talbot (2002) noted that certain groups of people most often succumb to epidemic hysteria—preadolescents and adolescents, especially, with girls more frequently affected than boys (p. 59).

Hacker/Sommers, *Working with Sources: Exercises for The Bedford Handbook*, 9th ed. (Boston: Bedford, 2014)

EXERCISE 59-3 ◆ Avoiding plagiarism in APA papers

To read about avoiding plagiarism, see 59 in *The Bedford Handbook*, Ninth Edition.

Read the following passage and the information about its source. Then decide whether each student sample is plagiarized or uses the source correctly. If the student sample is plagiarized, write "plagiarized"; if the sample is acceptable, write "OK."

ORIGINAL SOURCE

The dominant model of biological conservation everywhere is the national park: human exclusion from reserves designed for other species. The plausibility of this model arises from the fact that many extinctions are known to have been caused by human activities such as hunting, deforestation, and industrial pollution. During the last fifteen years, additional support has come from a new and highly fashionable science, conservation biology, which emerged in the United States in the 1980s. Devoted to the conservation of all biological diversity, rather than to the conservation and effective use of any specific resource, it is easily distinguishable from scientific forestry, fisheries biology, and so on, which nonetheless have some claim to be its intellectual antecedents.

From Sarkar, S. (2001). Restoring wilderness or reclaiming forests? In D. Rothenberg & M. Ulvaeus (Eds.), *The world and the wild* (pp. 37-55). Tucson: University of Arizona Press. [The source passage is from pages 37-38; only the last word appears on page 38.]

1. All over the world, the national park, which excludes humans from reserves designed for other species, is the dominant model of biological conservation.

2. S. Sarkar (2001) explained that national parks, which exclude humans from reserves designated for other species, are a plausible model of biological conservation because many extinctions are caused by deforestation, industrial pollution, hunting, and other human activities (p. 37).

3. According to Sarkar (2001), limiting human access to national parks has been a reasonable conservation technique because "many extinctions are known to have been caused by human activities such as hunting, deforestation, and industrial pollution" (p. 37).

4. Sarkar (2001) pointed out that the new science of conservation biology is "devoted to the conservation of all biological diversity, rather than to the conservation and effective use of any specific resource" (p. 37).

5. One writer has noted that conservation biology is focused on "the conservation of all biological diversity," whereas other conservation sciences focus on specific resources, such as forests or fisheries (Sarkar, 2001, p. 37).

Hacker/Sommers, *Working with Sources: Exercises for The Bedford Handbook*, 9th ed. (Boston: Bedford, 2014)

59-3 | Avoiding plagiarism in APA papers **55**

EXERCISE 59-4 ◆ Avoiding plagiarism in APA papers

To read about avoiding plagiarism, see 59 in *The Bedford Handbook*, Ninth Edition.

Read the following passage and the information about its source. Then decide whether each student sample is plagiarized or uses the source correctly. If the student sample is plagiarized, write "plagiarized"; if the sample is acceptable, write "OK."

ORIGINAL SOURCE

While Easter Island was divided into about eleven territories, each belonging to one clan under its own chief and competing with other clans, the island was also loosely integrated religiously, economically, and politically under the leadership of one paramount chief. On other Polynesian islands, competition between chiefs for prestige could take the form of inter-island efforts such as trading and raiding, but Easter's extreme isolation from other islands precluded that possibility. Instead, the excellent quality of Rano Raraku volcanic stone for carving eventually resulted in chiefs competing by erecting statues representing their high-ranking ancestors on rectangular stone platforms (termed *ahu*).

From Diamond, J. (2004, March 25). Twilight at Easter [Review of the books *The enigmas of Easter Island*, by J. Flenly & P. Bahn, and *Among stone giants: The life of Katherine Routledge and her remarkable expedition to Easter Island*, by J. A. Van Tilburg]. *New York Review of Books*, *51*(5), 6, 8-10. [The source paragraph appears on page 8.]

1. Diamond (2004) explained that the 11 territories on Easter Island were "loosely integrated religiously, economically, and politically" under the leadership of one paramount chief (p. 8).

2. Easter Island was more isolated than other Polynesian islands, and therefore its chiefs did not compete with chiefs from other islands, as was typical elsewhere in the South Pacific (Diamond, 2004, p. 8).

3. Diamond (2004) observed that "Easter Island was divided into about eleven territories, each belonging to one clan under its own chief and competing with other clans" (p. 8).

4. According to Diamond (2004), rivalries between Polynesian rulers for status sometimes took the form of island-to-island endeavors like commerce or invasions.

5. Diamond (2004) noted that rather than competing with chiefs on other Polynesian islands, Easter Island's chiefs competed among themselves by erecting statues representing their high-ranking ancestors.

Hacker/Sommers, *Working with Sources: Exercises for The Bedford Handbook*, 9th ed. (Boston: Bedford, 2014)

EXERCISE 59-5 ◆ Recognizing common knowledge in APA papers

To read about what constitutes common knowledge in the social sciences, see 59 in *The Bedford Handbook*, Ninth Edition.

Read the student passage and determine whether the student needs to cite the source of the information in an APA paper. If the material does not need citation because it is common knowledge, write "common knowledge." If the material is not common knowledge and the student should cite the source, write "needs citation."

EXAMPLE

Sigmund Freud believed that dreams provide clues about the dreamer's psychological conflicts. *Common Knowledge* [This general fact about Freud's ideas is widely known in the social sciences.]

1. In double-blind trials to test the effectiveness of St. John's wort as an antidepressant, the plant performed no better than a placebo.

2. In 2012, Ben Bernanke was the chair of the Federal Reserve Board.

3. In both 2011 and 2012, the most popular name given to baby girls in the United States was Sophia.

4. Phrenology, the study of bumps on the skull, advanced scientists' understanding of the ways different parts of the brain function.

5. The sense of smell and the sense of taste are linked.

6. When the Homestead Act took effect, granting 160 acres of western land to any head of a household—male or female—who would live there and improve it for five years, women filed 10% of the claims.

7. Babe Ruth's record for home runs in a single season was not broken for decades.

8. Many California earthquakes occur along the San Andreas Fault.

9. Studies have shown that unlike elderly Americans, who tend to become more forgetful as they age, elderly people in mainland China have memories as good as those of younger people in their culture.

10. Anorexia and bulimia are disorders affecting more young women than young men.

EXERCISE 60-1 ◆ Integrating sources in APA papers

To read about integrating sources, see 60 in *The Bedford Handbook*, Ninth Edition.

Read the following passage and the information about its source. Then decide whether each student sample uses the source correctly. If the student has made an error in using the source, revise the sample to avoid the error. If the student has quoted correctly, write "OK."

ORIGINAL SOURCE

Mental-health workers have long theorized that it takes grueling emotional exertion to recover from the death of a loved one. So-called grief work, now the stock-in-trade of a growing number of grief counselors, entails confronting the reality of a loved one's demise and grappling with the harsh emotions triggered by that loss.

Two new studies, however, knock grief work off its theoretical pedestal. Among bereaved spouses tracked for up to 2 years after their partners' death, those who often talked with others and briefly wrote in diaries about their emotions fared no better than their tight-lipped, unexpressive counterparts, according to psychologist Margaret Stroebe of Utrecht University in the Netherlands and her colleagues.

From Bower, B. (2002, March 2). Good grief: Bereaved adjust well without airing emotion. *Science News, 161*, 131-132. [The source passage is from page 131.]

1. Researchers at Utrecht University found that bereaved spouses who often talked with others and briefly wrote in diaries about their emotions fared no better than their tight-lipped, unexpressive counterparts (Bower, 2002, p. 131).

2. Researchers at Utrecht University found that bereaved spouses "who often talked with others and briefly wrote in diaries fared no better than their tight-lipped, unexpressive counterparts" (Bower, 2002, p. 131).

3. Psychologist Margaret Stroebe and her colleagues found that bereaved spouses "who often talked with others and briefly wrote in diaries . . . fared no better than their tight-lipped, unexpressive counterparts" (Bower, 2002, p. 131).

4. According to Bower (2002), "Mental-health workers have always believed that it takes grueling emotional exertion to recover from a loved one's death" (p. 131).

5. Mental health professionals have assumed that people stricken by grief need a great deal of help. "So-called grief work, now the stock-in-trade of a growing number of grief counselors, entails confronting the reality of a loved one's demise and grappling with the harsh emotions triggered by that loss" (Bower, 2002, p. 131).

6. Bower (2002) has observed that recent studies of bereaved spouses "knock grief work off its theoretical pedestal" (p. 131).

7. Bower (2002) has described grief counselors as helping the bereaved "[confront] the reality of a loved one's demise and [grapple] with the harsh emotions triggered by that loss" (p. 131).

Hacker/Sommers, *Working with Sources: Exercises for The Bedford Handbook*, 9th ed. (Boston: Bedford, 2014)

60-1 | Integrating sources in APA papers   **59**

8. Researchers at Utrecht University find no difference in the speed of adapting to a spouse's death among subjects "who often talked with others and briefly wrote in diaries" and "their tight-lipped, unexpressive counterparts" (Bower, 2002, p. 131).

9. Bower (2002) noted that new studies may change the common perception of how people recover from grief:

   "Among bereaved spouses tracked for up to 2 years after their partners' death, those who often talked with others and briefly wrote in diaries about their emotions fared no better than their tight-lipped, unexpressive counterparts, according to psychologist Margaret Stroebe of Utrecht University in the Netherlands and her colleagues." (p. 131)

10. "Mental-health workers have long theorized that it takes grueling emotional exertion to recover from the death of a loved one," reported Bower (2002), but "new studies . . . knock grief work off its theoretical pedestal" (p. 131).

Hacker/Sommers, *Working with Sources: Exercises for*
The Bedford Handbook, 9th ed. (Boston: Bedford, 2014)

EXERCISE 60-2 ◆ Integrating sources in APA papers

To read about integrating sources, see 60 in *The Bedford Handbook*, Ninth Edition.

Read the following passage and the information about its source. Then decide whether each student sample uses the source correctly. If the student has made an error in using the source, revise the sample to avoid the error. If the student has quoted correctly, write "OK."

ORIGINAL SOURCE

> Although convicted sex offenders raise justifiable concerns about public safety, studies indicate that many of them don't return to their criminal ways. Researchers are attempting to come up with statistical tools that courts can use to decide who should stay behind bars and who should go free.
>
> Data from several long-term studies of 4,724 sex offenders released from prisons in the United States and Canada after 1980 show that after 10 years, one in five had been arrested for a new sexual offense, says psychologist R. Karl Hanson of the Department of the Solicitor General of Canada in Ottawa. After 20 years, that figure rose to slightly more than one in four. Among men who had victimized children in their own families, an even lower fraction—about 1 in 10—committed a new sexual offense during the first 20 years after release from prison.
>
> Hanson, however, estimates that close to half the released sex offenders eventually commit another sex crime. "Most of their offenses are never reported to the authorities," he said.

From Bower, B. (2002, July 27). Men of prey. *Science News, 162,* 59-60. [The source passage is from page 60.]

1. According to Bower (2002), "Although convicted sex offenders raise justifiable concerns about public safety, studies indicate that many of them don't return to their criminal ways" (p. 60).

2. Bower (2002) reported a surprising finding based on several longitudinal studies: "Many convicted sex offenders don't return to their criminal ways" (p. 60).

3. No one has yet answered the question of how to deal with potentially dangerous sex offenders who are serving prison time. "Researchers are attempting to come up with statistical tools that courts can use to decide who should stay behind bars and who should go free" (Bower, 2002, p. 60).

4. Bower (2002) has suggested that scientists can help society decide how to deal with sex offenders: "Researchers are attempting to come up with statistical tools that courts can use to decide who should stay behind bars and who should go free" (p. 60).

5. A Canadian psychologist has reported that data from several long-term studies of 4,724 sex offenders released from prisons in the United States and Canada after 1980 show that after 10 years, one in five had been arrested for a new sexual offense (Bower, 2002, p. 60).

6. As Bower (2002) reported, studies of released sex offenders found that "after 10 years, one in five had been arrested for a new sexual offense. . . . After 20 years, that figure rose to slightly more than one in four" (p. 60).

Hacker/Sommers, *Working with Sources: Exercises for The Bedford Handbook,* 9th ed. (Boston: Bedford, 2014)

60-2 | Integrating sources in APA papers **61**

7. As long-term studies have indicated, "Among men who had victimized children in their own families, only about 10% committed a new sexual offense during the first 20 years after release from prison" (Bower, 2002, p. 60).

8. As Bower (2002) has noted, approximately 10% of men convicted of "victimiz[ing] children in their own families . . . committed a new sexual offense during the first 20 years after release from prison" (p. 60).

9. Bower (2002) provided evidence that sex offenders do not always repeat their crimes after serving sentences:

   > "Data from several long-term studies of 4,724 sex offenders released from prisons in the United States and Canada after 1980 show that after 10 years, one in five had been arrested for a new sexual offense, says psychologist R. Karl Hanson of the Department of the Solicitor General of Canada in Ottawa. After 20 years, that figure rose to slightly more than one in four." (p. 60)

10. Noting that the recidivism rates for sex offenders could be higher than the studies show, psychologist R. Karl Hanson explained, "Most of their offenses are never reported to the authorities" (as cited in Bower, 2002, p. 60).

Hacker/Sommers, *Working with Sources: Exercises for*
The Bedford Handbook, 9th ed. (Boston: Bedford, 2014)

EXERCISE 60-3 ◆ Integrating sources in APA papers

To read about integrating sources, see 60 in *The Bedford Handbook*, Ninth Edition.

Read the following passage and the information about its source. Then decide whether each student sample uses the source correctly. If the student has made an error in using the source, revise the sample to avoid the error. If the student has quoted correctly, write "OK."

ORIGINAL SOURCE

Like everyone else, teachers learn through experience, but they learn without much guidance. One problem, of course, is that experience, especially the kind that is both repetitious and disappointing, can easily harden into narrow pedagogical theories. Most schools have a teacher with a theory built on grudges. This teacher knows that there is just one way to conduct a lesson; she blames the children and their parents if the children don't catch on; she has a list of types and makes her students fit them; and she prides herself on her realism—most children come to school, she knows, to give her a hard time. Current research holds that most teachers get set in their ways, both their good and bad ones, after about four years of learning by experience. Many teachers don't last that long.

From Kidder, T. (1989). *Among schoolchildren.* Boston, MA: Houghton Mifflin. [The source passage is from page 51.]

1. According to Kidder, "teachers learn through experience, but they learn without much guidance" (1989, p. 51).

2. Kidder (1989) argued that teaching experience, "especially the kind that is repetitious and disappointing, easily hardens into narrow pedagogical theories" (p. 51).

3. Kidder (1989) has noted, "Current research holds that most teachers get set in their ways, both their good and bad ones, after about four years of learning by experience" (p. 51).

4. In the view of Kidder (1989), it's not unusual for a teacher "with a theory built on grudges" (p. 51).

5. Most teachers gain experience on the job and develop rigid habits and theories after as few as four years. "Many teachers don't last that long" (Kidder, 1989, p. 51).

Hacker/Sommers, *Working with Sources: Exercises for The Bedford Handbook*, 9th ed. (Boston: Bedford, 2014)

60-3 | Integrating sources in APA papers **63**

EXERCISE 60-4 ◆ Integrating sources in APA papers

To read about integrating sources, see 60 in *The Bedford Handbook*, Ninth Edition.

Read the following passage and the information about its source. Then decide whether each student sample uses the source correctly. If the student has made an error in using the source, revise the sample to avoid the error. If the student has quoted correctly, write "OK."

ORIGINAL SOURCE

Many policies on parenting . . . are inspired by research that finds a correlation between the behavior of parents and the behavior of children. Loving parents have confident children, authoritative parents (neither too permissive nor too punitive) have well-behaved children, parents who talk to their children have children with better language skills, and so on. Everyone concludes that to grow the best children, parents must be loving, authoritative, and talkative, and if children don't turn out well it must be the parents' fault. But the conclusions depend on the belief that children are blank slates. Parents, remember, provide their children with genes, not just a home environment. The correlations between parents and children may be telling us only that the same genes that make adults loving, authoritative, and talkative make their children self-confident, well-behaved, and articulate.

From Pinker, S. (2003). The blank slate: The modern denial of human nature. *Skeptical Inquirer, 27*(2), 37-41. [The source passage is from page 39.]

1. Pinker (2003) explained that much research on parenting "finds a correlation between the behavior of parents and the behavior of children" (p. 39).

2. Pinker (2003) has argued against the emphasis on the importance of a child's upbringing, noting, "Parents . . . provide their children with genes, not just a home environment" (p. 39).

3. Many people believe that the home environment has a direct effect on the way children grow up. "But the conclusions depend on the belief that children are blank slates" (Pinker, 2003, p. 39).

4. As Pinker (2003) has pointed out, "Everyone concludes that parents must be loving, authoritative, and talkative, and if children don't turn out well it must be the parents' fault. But the conclusions depend on the belief that children are blank slates" (p. 39).

5. Pinker (2003) pointed out that "children are blank slates" (p. 39).

64   60-4 | Integrating sources in APA papers

Hacker/Sommers, *Working with Sources: Exercises for The Bedford Handbook*, 9th ed. (Boston: Bedford, 2014)

EXERCISE 61-1 ◆ APA documentation: in-text citations

To read about how to use and format APA in-text citations, see 61a in *The Bedford Handbook*, Ninth Edition.

Circle the letter of the APA in-text citation that is handled correctly.

EXAMPLE

The student is quoting from page 49 of an article on parapsychology written by Peter Greasley and published in 2000.

(a.) Greasley (2000) noted, "It is relatively easy, with the benefit of a video recorder and a skeptical demeanor, to analyze the strategies used by the medium (consciously or not) to elicit a high ratio of positive response from the client" (p. 49).

b. Greasley (2000) noted, "It is relatively easy, with the benefit of a video recorder and a skeptical demeanor, to analyze the strategies used by the medium (consciously or not) to elicit a high ratio of positive response from the client" (49).

1. The student is quoting from page 26 of an article by Peter Greasley published in 2000.

   a. Greasley (2000) pointed out that clients who seek out mediums are so inclined to find the sessions impressive that "few can blame them for leaving the consultation expressing unequivocal satisfaction." (p. 26)

   b. Greasley (2000) pointed out that clients who seek out mediums are so inclined to find the sessions impressive that "few can blame them for leaving the consultation expressing unequivocal satisfaction" (p. 26).

2. The student is summarizing information from page 176 of a 1980 book with two authors, Marks and Kammann.

   a. The psychological phenomenon known as *selective exposure* occurs when people choose source material and authorities that reflect what they already believe (Marks & Kammann, 1980, p. 176).

   b. The psychological phenomenon known as *selective exposure* occurs when people choose source material and authorities that reflect what they already believe (Marks and Kammann, 1980, p. 176).

3. The student is quoting from page 29 of an article published in 2000 by Paul Kurtz.

   a. Kurtz has observed that "science has been investigating our ability to communicate with the dead for at least 150 years and it has attempted to discover empirical evidence in support of the claim" (2000, p. 29).

   b. Kurtz (2000) has observed that "science has been investigating our ability to communicate with the dead for at least 150 years and it has attempted to discover empirical evidence in support of the claim" (p. 29).

Hacker/Sommers, *Working with Sources: Exercises for The Bedford Handbook*, 9th ed. (Boston: Bedford, 2014)

61-1 | APA documentation: in-text citations **65**

4. The student is summarizing information from a 2001 article by Gary E. R. Schwartz, Linda G. S. Russek, Lonnie A. Nelson, and Christopher Barentsen. This is the first citation of the source in the paper.

   a. Schwartz et al. (2001) insisted that the study had eliminated fraud and coincidence as possible explanations for the success of the mediums tested.

   b. Schwartz, Russek, Nelson, and Barentsen (2001) insisted that the study had eliminated fraud and coincidence as possible explanations for the success of the mediums tested.

5. The student is quoting from page 27 of an article by two authors, Wiseman and O'Keeffe, that was published in 2001.

   a. According to Wiseman and O'Keeffe (2001), "The Schwartz et al. studies suffered from severe methodological problems, namely: (1) the potential for judging bias, (2) the use of an inappropriate control group, and (3) inadequate safeguards against sensory leakage" (p. 27).

   b. According to Wiseman & O'Keeffe (2001), "The Schwartz et al. studies suffered from severe methodological problems, namely: (1) the potential for judging bias, (2) the use of an inappropriate control group, and (3) inadequate safeguards against sensory leakage" (p. 27).

6. The student is quoting from page 52 of a 2001 article, "Talking to the Dead," by Leon Jaroff. The list of references contains another article, "The Man Who Loves to Bust Quacks," also written by Jaroff and also published in 2001.

   a. Jaroff (2001b) claimed that the medium used "a sophisticated form of the game Twenty Questions, during which the subject, anxious to hear from the dead, seldom realizes that he, not the medium or the departed, is supplying the answers" (p. 52).

   b. Jaroff (2001) claimed that the medium used "a sophisticated form of the game Twenty Questions, during which the subject, anxious to hear from the dead, seldom realizes that he, not the medium or the departed, is supplying the answers" ("Talking to the Dead," p. 52).

7. The student is quoting from paragraph 1 of a 1998 online article by Travis Dacolias. The article has numbered paragraphs but no page numbers.

   a. Dacolias (1998) noted, "Cold reading is a technique used by tarot card readers, psychics, palm readers, astrologers, and even con men to get people to believe that the cold reader knows all about them, even though they have never met" (para. 1).

   b. Dacolias (1998) noted, "Cold reading is a technique used by tarot card readers, psychics, palm readers, astrologers, and even con men to get people to believe that the cold reader knows all about them, even though they have never met."

Hacker/Sommers, *Working with Sources: Exercises for The Bedford Handbook*, 9th ed. (Boston: Bedford, 2014)

8. The student is summarizing information from an undated online article by Ray Hyman. The article has no paragraph or page numbers.

   a. Hyman pointed out that no medium has ever managed to demonstrate psychic abilities under controlled laboratory conditions, even though large cash prizes have been offered to anyone who succeeds.

   b. Hyman (n.d.) pointed out that no medium has ever managed to demonstrate psychic abilities under controlled laboratory conditions, even though large cash prizes have been offered to anyone who succeeds.

9. The student is quoting from page 12 of a 2000 report by the National Science Board. No individual author is given. The entry in the list of references begins like this: National Science Board.

   a. The National Science Board (2000) cautioned that believers in paranormal phenomena are dangerously distanced from reality: "Their beliefs may indicate an absence of critical thinking skills necessary not only for informed decisionmaking in the voting booth and other civic venues (for example, jury duty), but also for making wise choices needed for everyday living" (p. 12).

   b. The National Science Board cautioned that believers in paranormal phenomena are dangerously distanced from reality: "Their beliefs may indicate an absence of critical thinking skills necessary not only for informed decisionmaking in the voting booth and other civic venues (for example, jury duty), but also for making wise choices needed for everyday living" (Anonymous, 2000, p. 12).

10. The student is summarizing information that begins on page 29 and continues on page 30 in a 2000 article by Paul Kurtz.

    a. Kurtz (2000) argued that mediums claiming to communicate with the dead were aided at the end of the twentieth century by mass media exposure and a credulous American public (pp. 29-30).

    b. Kurtz (2000) argued that mediums claiming to communicate with the dead were aided at the end of the twentieth century by mass media exposure and a credulous American public (pp. 29+).

Hacker/Sommers, *Working with Sources: Exercises for*
The Bedford Handbook, 9th ed. (Boston: Bedford, 2014)

61-1 | APA documentation: in-text citations   **67**

EXERCISE 61-2 ◆ APA documentation: in-text citations

To read about how to use and format APA in-text citations, see 61a in *The Bedford Handbook*, Ninth Edition.

Circle the letter of the APA in-text citation that is handled correctly.

EXAMPLE

The student is quoting from page 96 of a book, *How to Have a Smarter Baby*, written by Susan Ludington-Hoe and Susan K. Golant and published in 1985.

a. Ludington-Hoe (1985) noted that music "has been known to stimulate the brain's right side (fostering creativity) and actually help babies gain more weight and cry less" (p. 96).

b. Ludington-Hoe and Golant (1985) noted that music "has been known to stimulate the brain's right side (fostering creativity) and actually help babies gain more weight and cry less" (p. 96).

1. The student is quoting from page 406 of a book by Benjamin Spock that was published in 1965.

   a. Spock (1965) warned ambitious parents decades ago to "be on guard against using their ambition to run their children's lives" (406).

   b. Spock (1965) warned ambitious parents decades ago to "be on guard against using their ambition to run their children's lives" (p. 406).

2. The student is summarizing information from page 152 of a 1985 book with two authors, Susan Ludington-Hoe and Susan K. Golant.

   a. Some specialists in infant development have urged parents to stimulate newborns immediately after birth by placing black-and-white pictures near their faces (Ludington-Hoe & Golant, 1985, p. 152).

   b. Some specialists in infant development have urged parents to stimulate newborns immediately after birth by placing black-and-white pictures near their faces (Ludington-Hoe and Golant, 1985, p. 152).

3. The student is quoting from page 121 of a 1997 book by Signe Larson and Kevin Osborn.

   a. Larson and Osborn (1997) asserted that talking, singing, and reading "can all encourage the development of [an] infant's language and communication skills" (p. 121).

   b. Larson & Osborn (1997) asserted that talking, singing, and reading "can all encourage the development of [an] infant's language and communication skills" (p. 121).

4. The student is quoting a paginated online article by Karen Karbo published in 2000.

   a. Karbo (2000) pointed out that *parenting* "became a verb only around 1960" (p. 2).

   b. Karbo (2000) pointed out that *parenting* "became a verb only around 1960."

Hacker/Sommers, *Working with Sources: Exercises for The Bedford Handbook*, 9th ed. (Boston: Bedford, 2014)

61-2 | APA documentation: in-text citations **69**

5. The student is summarizing information from an article, "Talks of a Reluctant Parenting Pundit," by Katie Allison Granju, which was published in 1999. The list of references includes another article, "Formula for Disaster," also written by Granju and also published in 1999.

   a. Granju (1999) has explained that even those who write about parent-child relationships can sometimes feel that they are ineffective parents to their own children ("Talks").

   b. Granju (1999b) has explained that even those who write about parent-child relationships can sometimes feel that they are ineffective parents to their own children.

6. The student is quoting from a 1999 report by the National Institute of Child Health and Human Development; the author is unnamed. The report appeared on an unpaginated Web site, and the quoted words appeared in the sixth paragraph under the heading "Children Score Higher."

   a. The National Institute of Child Health and Human Development (1999) has found that "children fared better when child-staff ratios [in child care centers] were lower, and also when teachers had more training and education" (Children Score Higher section, para. 6).

   b. The National Institute of Child Health and Human Development (1999) has found that "children fared better when child-staff ratios [in child care centers] were lower, and also when teachers had more training and education" (para. 6).

7. The student is quoting from page F8 of a 2002 newspaper article by Eric Nagourney.

   a. In many cases, as Nagourney (2002) has observed, "The competition to get children into the best schools begins before they start kindergarten" (p. F8).

   b. In many cases, as Nagourney (2002) has observed, "The competition to get children into the best schools begins before they start kindergarten." (p. F8)

8. The student is quoting from an article by Don Campbell on a Web site without pagination but with numbered paragraphs. The quotation was taken from the Frequently Asked Questions section, paragraph 9, and the Web site was last updated in 2002.

   a. On his website, Campbell has claimed that "students who listened to Mozart prior to testing scored higher marks in an intelligence test" (2002, Frequently Asked Questions section, para. 9).

   b. On his website, Campbell (2002) has claimed that "students who listened to Mozart prior to testing scored higher marks in an intelligence test" (Frequently Asked Questions section, para. 9).

9. The writer is quoting from page 366 of a 1999 journal article by Kenneth M. Steele, Karen E. Bass, and Melissa D. Crook. This is the first citation of the source in the paper.

   a. Steele, Bass, and Crook (1999) noted that "several attempts by other laboratories to confirm the existence of a Mozart effect have been unsuccessful" (p. 366).

   b. Steele et al. (1999) noted that "several attempts by other laboratories to confirm the existence of a Mozart effect have been unsuccessful" (p. 366).

Hacker/Sommers, *Working with Sources: Exercises for The Bedford Handbook*, 9th ed. (Boston: Bedford, 2014)

10. The student is summarizing material from an article by Eric Chudler on an undated Web site with no page numbers.

    a. Chudler (n.d.) noted that the original Mozart studies were never intended to measure how a baby's intelligence might be affected by classical music.

    b. Chudler noted that the original Mozart studies were never intended to measure how a baby's intelligence might be affected by classical music.

Hacker/Sommers, *Working with Sources: Exercises for* *The Bedford Handbook*, 9th ed. (Boston: Bedford, 2014)

61-2 | APA documentation: in-text citations   **71**

EXERCISE 61-3 ◆ APA documentation: in-text citations

To read about how to use and format APA in-text citations, see 61a in *The Bedford Handbook*, Ninth Edition.

Circle the letter of the APA in-text citation that is handled correctly.

EXAMPLE

The writer is quoting from page 543 of the following book:

Myers, D. G. (2002). *Exploring psychology* (5th ed.). Boston, MA: Worth.

(a.) As one discussion of Milgram's obedience studies points out, "great evils sometimes grow out of people's compliance with lesser evils" (Myers, 2002, p. 543).

b. As one discussion of Milgram's obedience studies points out, "great evils sometimes grow out of people's compliance with lesser evils" (Myers, p. 543).

1. The student is paraphrasing the following newspaper article:

   Schwartz, J. (2004, May 6). Simulated prison in '71 showed a fine line between "normal" and "monster." *The New York Times*, p. A20.

   a. Schwartz (2004, May 6) reported on a psychology experiment in 1971 in which volunteers were randomly assigned to be either prison guards or prisoners. Those who became guards quickly turned abusive toward their prisoners, and the experiment was stopped a week ahead of schedule.

   b. Schwartz (2004) reported on a psychology experiment in 1971 in which volunteers were randomly assigned to be either prison guards or prisoners. Those who became guards quickly turned abusive toward their prisoners, and the experiment was stopped a week ahead of schedule.

2. The student is quoting from page 495 of the following book:

   Hockenbury, D. M., & Hockenbury, S. E. (2000). *Psychology* (2nd ed.). New York, NY: Worth.

   a. According to one psychology text, Milgram's experiment was designed to answer the question "Could a person be pressured by others into committing an immoral act, some action that violated his or her own conscience, such as hurting a stranger?" (Hockenbury & Hockenbury, 2000, p. 495).

   b. According to one psychology text, Milgram's experiment was designed to answer the question "Could a person be pressured by others into committing an immoral act, some action that violated his or her own conscience, such as hurting a stranger?" (Hockenbury and Hockenbury, 2000, p. 495).

3. The student is quoting from page A20 of the following newspaper article:

   Dao, J., & von Zielbauer, P. (2004, May 6). Abuse charges bring anguish in unit's home. *The New York Times*, pp. A1, A20.

   a. Dao and von Zielbauer (2004) reported that one accused soldier "told military investigators that her job was 'to keep detainees awake'" (p. A1+).

   b. Dao and von Zielbauer (2004) reported that one accused soldier "told military investigators that her job was 'to keep detainees awake'" (p. A20).

Hacker/Sommers, *Working with Sources: Exercises for The Bedford Handbook*, 9th ed. (Boston: Bedford, 2014)

61-3 | APA documentation: in-text citations **73**

4. The student used two sources by the same author published in the same year. The sources appear as follows in the reference list:

    Hersh, S. M. (2004a, May 17). Chain of command. *The New Yorker, 80*(12), 38-43.

    Hersh, S. M. (2004b, May 10). Torture at Abu Ghraib. *The New Yorker, 80*(11), 42-47.

    The writer is quoting from page 43 of the article "Chain of Command."

    a. Hersh (2004) said, "The photographing of prisoners . . . seems to have been not random but, rather, part of the dehumanizing interrogation process" ("Chain of Command," p. 43).

    b. Hersh (2004a) said, "The photographing of prisoners . . . seems to have been not random but, rather, part of the dehumanizing interrogation process" (p. 43).

5. The writer is summarizing material from page 67 of the following book:

    Nevid, J. S., Rathus, S. A., & Rubenstein, H. R. (1998). *Health in the new millennium.* New York, NY: Worth.

    This is the second citation of the book in the paper.

    a. Nevid et al. (1998) pointed out that people who have had traumatic experiences may later suffer from post-traumatic stress disorder, or PTSD (p. 67).

    b. Nevid, Rathus, and Rubenstein (1998) pointed out that people who have had traumatic experiences may later suffer from post-traumatic stress disorder, or PTSD (p. 67).

Hacker/Sommers, *Working with Sources: Exercises for The Bedford Handbook*, 9th ed. (Boston: Bedford, 2014)

EXERCISE 61-4 ◆ APA documentation: identifying elements of sources

To read about how to handle the elements of sources in APA citations, see 61b in *The Bedford Handbook*, Ninth Edition.

Circle the correct answer for each question using information in the source provided.

SOURCE: AN EDITION OTHER THAN THE FIRST

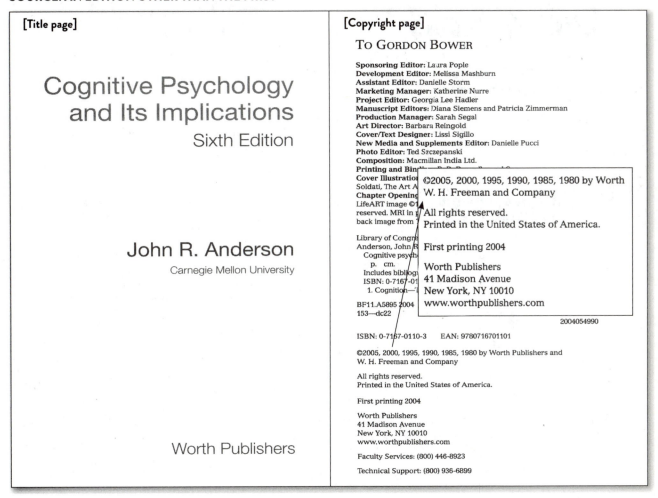

1. How would you begin an APA reference list entry for this source?

   a. Anderson, J. R. (2005).

   b. Anderson, J. R. (1980).

2. How would you cite the title and publisher for this source in an APA reference list entry?

   a. *Cognitive Psychology and Its Implications*. New York, NY: Worth.

   b. *Cognitive psychology and its implications* (6th ed.). New York, NY: Worth.

Hacker/Sommers, *Working with Sources: Exercises for The Bedford Handbook*, 9th ed. (Boston: Bedford, 2014)

61-4 | APA documentation: identifying elements of sources   **75**

[Title page]

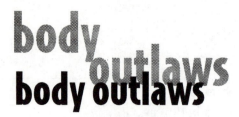

body outlaws

**rewriting the rules
of beauty and body image**

edited by ophira edut
foreword by rebecca walker

seal press

[First page of chapter]

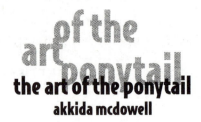

the art of the ponytail
akkida mcdowell

My crowning glory is a war zone. Every day I wake up prepared to do battle, to fight both for and against the enemy that lies on top of my head.

For years, I clashed with my hair. I struggled to make it mind my fingers. I flip-flopped over the best direction to take with it. From outside sources, I got the message: If my hair didn't look good (to them), I wasn't any good. My hair dictated whether I went out or not. On days that my hair acted up, the TV kept me company. According to movies, my beloved television, my classmates and even my neighbors, a proper hairstyle not only completed the package, but defined and delivered it.

When my hairstyle differed from the elaborate norm, my classmates and peers viewed me as unacceptable. My search for simple hairstyles in the realm of celebrities, newscasters, billboards and family proved futile. Even perusing the aisles for hair care products

124

3. You have used the chapter on the right from the collection whose title page is on the left. What information would come first in your APA reference list entry?

   a. McDowell, A.

   b. Edut, O. (Ed.).

4. What is the correct APA reference list entry for this source? The book was published in Emeryville, California, in 2003; the chapter begins on page 124 and ends on page 132.

   a. Edut, O. (Ed.). (2003). *Body Outlaws: Rewriting the Rules of Beauty and Body Image* (pp. 124-132). Emeryville, CA: Seal Press.

   b. McDowell, A. (2003). The art of the ponytail. In O. Edut (Ed.), *Body outlaws: Rewriting the rules of beauty and body image* (pp. 124-132). Emeryville, CA: Seal Press.

76 **61-4** | APA documentation: identifying elements of sources

Hacker/Sommers, *Working with Sources: Exercises for The Bedford Handbook*, 9th ed. (Boston: Bedford, 2014)

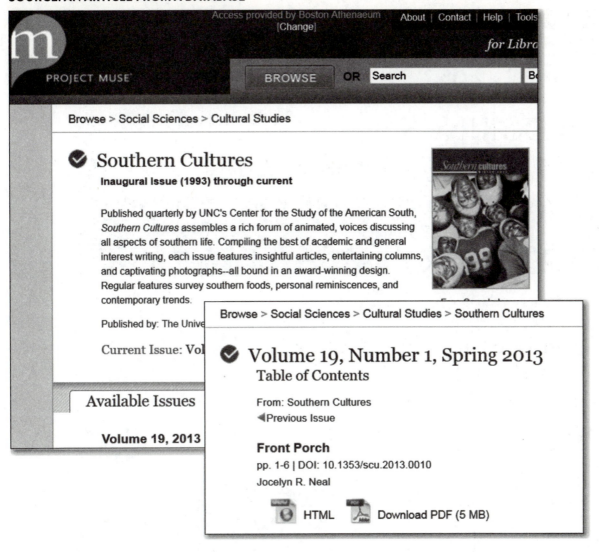

5. How would you begin an APA reference list entry for this article from a database?

   a. Neal, J. R. (2013). Front porch.

   b. Neal, J. R. (2013). "Front porch."

6. How would you cite the publication information for the periodical in this database record? (Each issue of the volume begins on page 1.)

   a. *Southern Cultures, 19*(1), 1-6.

   b. *Southern Cultures, 19* (2013): 1-6.

7. How would you end the reference list entry for this source?

   a. Retrieved from Project Muse database (doi:10.1353/scu.2013.0010).

   b. doi:10.1353/scu.2013.0010

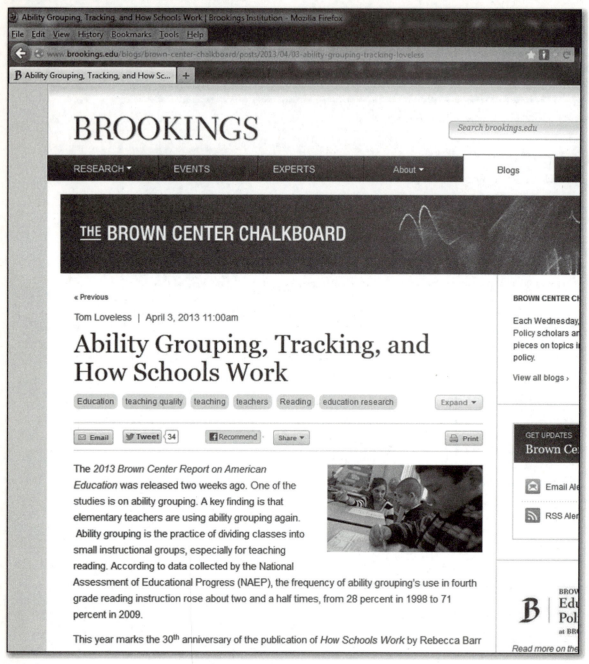

8. What is the correct APA reference list entry for this blog post on a Web site?

    a. Loveless, T. (2013, April 3). *Ability grouping, tracking, and how schools work*. Retrieved from
        http://brookings.edu/blogs/brown-center-chalkboard/posts/2013/04 /03-ability-grouping
        -tracking-loveless

    b. Loveless, T. (2013, April 3). Ability grouping, tracking, and how schools work [Blog post].
        Retrieved from http://www.brookings.edu/blogs/brown-center-chalkboard/posts/2013/04
        /03-ability-grouping-tracking-loveless

SOURCE: AN ARTICLE IN A MAGAZINE

[Table of contents]

[First page of article]

9. How would you cite the title of this article in an APA reference list entry?

    a. Insights: When medicine meets literature.

    b. When medicine meets literature.

10. What is the correct APA reference list entry for this source? (The article appears on pages 38 and 39 in the magazine.)

    a. Holloway, M. (2005, May). When medicine meets literature. *Scientific American, 292*(5), 38-39.

    b. Holloway, M. (2005). When medicine meets literature. *Scientific American, 292*(5), 38-39.

EXERCISE 61-5 ◆ APA documentation: reference list

To read about how to create and format an APA reference list, see 61b in *The Bedford Handbook*, Ninth Edition.

Circle the letter of the APA reference list entry that is handled correctly.

EXAMPLE

The student has quoted from a book, *Tapped: The Coming World Crisis in Water and What We Can Do about It*, by Paul Simon. It was published in New York in 1998 by Welcome Rain Publishers.

a. Simon, Paul. (1998). *Tapped: The coming world crisis in water and what we can do about it.* New York, NY: Welcome Rain.

(b.) Simon, P. (1998). *Tapped: The coming world crisis in water and what we can do about it.* New York, NY: Welcome Rain.

1. The student has included material from a book, *Water Wars: Drought, Flood, Folly, and the Politics of Thirst*, by Diane Raines Ward. It was published in New York by Riverhead Books in 2002.

    a. Ward, D. R. (2002). *Water Wars: Drought, Flood, Folly, and the Politics of Thirst.* New York, NY: Riverhead Books.

    b. Ward, D. R. (2002). *Water wars: Drought, flood, folly, and the politics of thirst.* New York, NY: Riverhead Books.

2. The student has paraphrased material from a book, *Blue Gold: The Fight to Stop the Corporate Theft of the World's Water*, by Maude Barlow and Tony Clarke. It was published in 2003 in New York by New Press.

    a. Barlow, M., & T. Clarke. (2003). *Blue gold: The fight to stop the corporate theft of the world's water.* New York, NY: New Press.

    b. Barlow, M., & Clarke, T. (2003). *Blue gold: The fight to stop the corporate theft of the world's water.* New York, NY: New Press.

3. The student has cited an article, "Survival of Fishes after Impingement on Traveling Screens at Hudson River Power Plants," by Paul H. Muessig, Jay B. Hutchinson Jr., Lawrence R. King, Rebecca J. Ligotino, and Martin Daley. The article appears in the book *Science, Law, and Hudson River Power Plants*, edited by Lawrence W. Barnthouse, Ronald J. Klauda, Douglas S. Vaughan, and Robert L. Kendall. The book was published in Bethesda, Maryland, by American Fisheries Society in 1998.

    a. Muessig, P. H., Hutchinson, J. B., Jr., King, L. R., Ligotino, R. J., & Daley, M. (1998). Survival of fishes after impingement on traveling screens at Hudson River power plants. In L. W. Barnthouse, R. J. Klauda, D. S. Vaughan, & R. L. Kendall (Eds.), *Science, law, and Hudson River power plants.* Bethesda, MD: American Fisheries Society.

Hacker/Sommers, *Working with Sources: Exercises for The Bedford Handbook*, 9th ed. (Boston: Bedford, 2014)

61-5 | APA documentation: reference list **81**

b. Muessig, P. H., et al. (1998). Survival of fishes after impingement on traveling screens at Hudson River power plants. In L. W. Barnthouse, R. J. Klauda, D. S. Vaughan, & R. L. Kendall (Eds.), *Science, law, and Hudson River power plants.* Bethesda, MD: American Fisheries Society.

4. The student has summarized material from an article, "Drought Settles In, Lake Shrinks, and West's Worries Grow," by Kirk Johnson and Dean E. Murphy. The article appears on pages 1 and 33 of the May 2, 2004, issue of *The New York Times.*

   a. Johnson, K., & Murphy, D. E. (2004, May 2). Drought settles in, lake shrinks, and West's worries grow. *The New York Times,* pp. 1, 33.

   b. Johnson, K., & Murphy, D. E. (2004, May 2). Drought settles in, lake shrinks, and West's worries grow. *The New York Times,* pp. 1+.

5. The student has quoted from a book, *Water Wars: Privatization, Pollution, and Profit,* by Vandana Shiva. It was published in 2002 in Cambridge, Massachusetts, by South End Press. The paper cites another book by Shiva from the same year, *Protect or Plunder? Understanding Intellectual Property Rights.*

   a. Shiva, V. (2002b). *Water wars: Privatization, pollution, and profit.* Cambridge, MA: South End Press.

   b. Shiva, V. (2002a). *Water wars: Privatization, pollution, and profit.* Cambridge, MA: South End Press.

6. The paper cites an article, "Tales of the Undammed," by Edna Francisco. It appears on pages 235-237 of the April 10, 2004, edition of the magazine *Science News* (volume 165, issue 15). The magazine is paginated continuously throughout the volume.

   a. Francisco, E. (2004, April 10). Tales of the undammed. *Science News, 165,* 235-237.

   b. Francisco, E. (2004, April 10). Tales of the undammed. *Science News, 165*(15), 235-237.

7. The paper cites an article, "Not a Drop to Drink," by Suzy Hansen, from the online magazine *Salon.com* (home page http://www.salon.com/). The article is dated August 28, 2002, and is at the URL http://dir.salon.com/story/books/int/2002/08/28/ward/index.html.

   a. Hansen, S. (2002, August 28). Not a drop to drink. *Salon.com.* Retrieved from http://dir.salon.com/story/books/int/2002/08/28/ward/index.html

   b. Hansen, S. (2002, August 28). Not a drop to drink. *Salon.com.* Retrieved from http://www.salon.com/

8. The paper includes material from an article titled "Water: An Imminent Global Crisis," written by Fred Pearce and published in the periodical *Geographical* in 2004 (volume 76, issue 8) on pages 34-36. The writer accessed the article using the InfoTrac database (article number A120128508). The writer also found the *Geographical* home page at http://www.geographical.co.uk/.

   a. Pearce, F. (2004). Water: An imminent global crisis. *Geographical, 76*(8), 34-36. Retrieved from http://www.geographical.co.uk/

   b. Pearce, F. (2004). Water: An imminent global crisis. *Geographical, 76*(8), 34-36. Retrieved from InfoTrac database. (A120128508)

9. The paper cites a review of a book, *Water Wars: Drought, Flood, Folly, and the Politics of Thirst*, by Diane Raines Ward. The review, titled "Over the Dam," was written by Ann Finkbeiner on October 27, 2002. The writer retrieved the article on the Web site of *The New York Times*, http://nytimes.com/.

   a. Finkbeiner, A. (2002, October 27). Over the dam [Review of the book *Water wars: Drought, flood, folly, and the politics of thirst*, by D. R. Ward]. *The New York Times.* Retrieved from http://nytimes.com/

   b. Finkbeiner, A. (2002, October 27). Over the dam. *The New York Times.* Retrieved from http://nytimes.com/

10. The paper includes a quotation from an e-mail message sent to the writer by Diane Raines Ward. It was received on May 23, 2004.

   a. Ward, D. R. (2004, May 23). Personal communication.

   b. No entry in the reference list

Hacker/Sommers, *Working with Sources: Exercises for The Bedford Handbook*, 9th ed. (Boston: Bedford, 2014)

61-5 | APA documentation: reference list **83**

EXERCISE 61-6 ◆ APA documentation: reference list

To read about how to create and format an APA reference list, see 61b in *The Bedford Handbook*, Ninth Edition.

Circle the letter of the APA reference list entry that is handled correctly.

EXAMPLE

The student has summarized information from the book *The Longevity Revolution: The Benefits and Challenges of Living a Long Life*, by Robert N. Butler. The book was published in New York in 2008 by PublicAffairs.

a. Butler, R. N. *The longevity revolution: The benefits and challenges of living a long life.* New York, NY: PublicAffairs, 2008.

b. Butler, R. N. (2008). *The longevity revolution: The benefits and challenges of living a long life.* New York, NY: PublicAffairs.

1. The student has summarized material from a document titled "Inside the Brain: An Interactive Tour" on the Alzheimer's Association Web site. The copyright date for the article is 2008, and there is no named author. The URL is http://www.alz.org/alzheimers_disease_4719 .asp.

   a. *Inside the brain: An interactive tour.* (2008). Retrieved from http://www.alz.org/alzheimers _disease_4719.asp

   b. Alzheimer's Association. (2008). *Inside the brain: An interactive tour.* Retrieved from http://www.alz .org/alzheimers_disease_4719.asp

2. The student has quoted from a documentary DVD titled *The Forgetting: A Portrait of Alzheimer's*, dated 2004. Elizabeth Arledge is listed as the producer and director, and Warner Home Video, in Burbank, California, is the distributor.

   a. Arledge, E., Producer/director. (2004). *The forgetting: A portrait of Alzheimer's* [DVD]. Burbank, CA: Warner Home Video.

   b. Arledge, E. (Producer/director). (2004). *The forgetting: A portrait of Alzheimer's* [DVD]. Burbank, CA: Warner Home Video.

3. The student has paraphrased an article by Joseph Nocera, "Taking Science Personally," found on page F1 in *The New York Times*, November 11, 2008.

   a. Nocera, J. (2008, November 11). Taking science personally. *The New York Times*, p. F1.

   b. Nocera, J. (2008, November 11). Taking science personally. *The New York Times*, F1.

4. The student has quoted material from page 320 of an article in volume 43, issue 3, of the *British Journal of Clinical Psychology*. The article, "Life Events, Depression, and Social Support in Dementia," was published in September 2004 and is printed on pages 313-324. The journal is paginated continuously throughout the volume. The authors are Allyson Waite, Paul Bebbington, Martin Skelton-Robinson, and Martin Orrell.

Hacker/Sommers, *Working with Sources: Exercises for The Bedford Handbook*, 9th ed. (Boston: Bedford, 2014)

61-6 | APA documentation: reference list   **85**

a.   Waite, A., Bebbington, P., Skelton-Robinson, M., & Orrell, M. (2004). Life events, depression, and social support in dementia. *British Journal of Clinical Psychology, 43,* 313-324.

b.   Waite, A., Bebbington, P., Skelton-Robinson, M., & Orrell, M. (2004). Life events, depression, and social support in dementia. *British Journal of Clinical Psychology, 43,* 320.

5.   The student has summarized information from the book *Aging, Biotechnology, and the Future,* edited by Catherine Y. Read, Robert C. Green, and Michael A. Smyer. The book was published in Baltimore, Maryland, in 2008 by Johns Hopkins University Press.

a.   Read, C. Y., Green, R. C., & Smyer, M. A. (Eds.). (2008). *Aging, biotechnology, and the future.* Baltimore, MD: Johns Hopkins University Press.

b.   Read, C. Y., Green, R. C., & Smyer, M. A. (2008). *Aging, biotechnology, and the future.* Baltimore, MD: Johns Hopkins University Press.

6.   The student has quoted material from an article, "Behavioral Medicine and Aging," in the *Journal of Consulting and Clinical Psychology,* accessed in the PsycARTICLES database. The article was published in volume 70, issue 3, in June 2002, on pages 843-851. The journal is paginated continuously throughout the volume. The article was written by Ilene C. Siegler, Lori A. Bastian, David C. Steffens, Hayden B. Bosworth, and Paul T. Costa. The database provides the DOI (digital object identifier) 10.1037/0022-006X.70.3.843 for the article.

a.   Siegler, I. C., Bastian, L. A., Steffens, D. C., Bosworth, H. B., & Costa, P. T. (2002). Behavioral medicine and aging. *Journal of Consulting and Clinical Psychology, 70,* 843-851. Retrieved from PsycARTICLES database. doi:10.1037/0022-006X.70.3.843

b.   Siegler, I. C., Bastian, L. A., Steffens, D. C., Bosworth, H. B., & Costa, P. T. (2002). Behavioral medicine and aging. *Journal of Consulting and Clinical Psychology, 70,* 843-851. doi:10.1037/0022-006X.70.3.843

7.   The student has paraphrased material from an article titled "The Role of Coping Humor in the Physical and Mental Health of Older Adults," published in November 2008 in the scholarly journal *Aging and Mental Health,* volume 12, issue 6, pages 713-718. The journal is paginated continuously throughout the volume. The article was written by Elsa Marziali, Lynn McDonald, and Peter Donahue.

a.   Marziali, E., McDonald, L., & Donahue, P. (2008). The role of coping humor in the physical and mental health of older adults. *Aging and Mental Health, 12,* 713-718.

b.   Marziali, E., McDonald, L., & Donahue, P. (2008, November). The role of coping humor in the physical and mental health of older adults. *Aging and Mental Health, 12,* 713-718.

8. The student summarized information from an audio file that was retrieved from the Web site http://www.npr.org/templates/story/story.php?storyId=99958952. The story, "Brain Study Indicates Why Some Memories Persist," was reported by Jon Hamilton and posted on January 29, 2009. It was retrieved by the student on February 8, 2009.

   a. Hamilton, J. (2008, January 29). Brain study indicates why some memories persist [Audio file]. Retrieved February 8, 2009, from http://www.npr.org/templates/story/story.php ?storyId=99958952

   b. Hamilton, J. (2008, January 29). Brain study indicates why some memories persist [Audio file]. Retrieved from http://www.npr.org/templates/story/story.php?storyId=99958952

9. The student has paraphrased information from an abstract of a journal article titled "Aging and Emotional Memory: Cognitive Mechanisms Underlying the Positivity Effect." The article was written by Julia Spaniol, Andreas Voss, and Cheryl L. Grady and appears on pages 859-872 of volume 23, issue 4, of *Psychology and Aging*, published in December 2008. The journal is paginated continuously throughout the volume.

   a. Spaniol, J., Voss, A., & Grady, C. L. (2008). Abstract of Aging and emotional memory: Cognitive mechanisms underlying the positivity effect. *Psychology and Aging, 23*, 859-872.

   b. Spaniol, J., Voss, A., & Grady, C. L. (2008). Aging and emotional memory: Cognitive mechanisms underlying the positivity effect [Abstract]. *Psychology and Aging, 23*, 859-872.

10. The student is quoting material from a doctoral dissertation by Lea Angela Truman Drye titled *Examining the Relationship of Education and Late-Life Mental Activity with Cognitive Decline*, dated 2008. The dissertation was retrieved from the ProQuest Dissertations and Theses database and has the accession number AAT 3309643.

   a. Drye, L. A. T. (2008). *Examining the relationship of education and late-life mental activity with cognitive decline* (Doctoral dissertation). Available from ProQuest Dissertations and Theses database. (AAT 3309643)

   b. Drye, L. A. T. (2008). *Examining the relationship of education and late-life mental activity with cognitive decline*. Available from ProQuest Dissertations and Theses database.

Hacker/Sommers, *Working with Sources: Exercises for The Bedford Handbook*, 9th ed. (Boston: Bedford, 2014)

61-6 | APA documentation: reference list   **87**

EXERCISE 61-7 ◆ APA documentation: reference list

To read about how to create and format an APA reference list, see 61b in *The Bedford Handbook*, Ninth Edition.

Circle the letter of the APA reference list entry that is handled correctly.

EXAMPLE

The student has summarized information from the article "Patterns of Parent-Reported Homework Problems among ADHD-referred and Non-referred Children." The article was written by Thomas J. Power, Branlyn E. Werba, Marley W. Watkins, Jennifer G. Angelucci, and Ricardo B. Eiraldi, and it appeared on pages 13-33 of volume 21, issue 1, of *School Psychology Quarterly* in 2006. The journal is paginated continuously throughout the volume.

a. Power, T. J., Werba, B. E., Watkins, M. W., Angelucci, J. G., & Eiraldi, R. B. (2006). Patterns of parent-reported homework problems among ADHD-referred and non-referred children. *School Psychology Quarterly, 21*.

(b.) Power, T. J., Werba, B. E., Watkins, M. W., Angelucci, J. G., & Eiraldi, R. B. (2006). Patterns of parent-reported homework problems among ADHD-referred and non-referred children. *School Psychology Quarterly, 21*, 13-33.

1. The student has summarized material from a government report titled *Teaching Children with Attention Deficit Hyperactivity Disorder: Instructional Strategies and Practices, 2008*, which was written and published in Washington, DC, in 2008 by the U.S. Department of Education.

   a. U.S. Department of Education. (2008). *Teaching children with attention deficit hyperactivity disorder: Instructional strategies and practices, 2008*. Washington, DC: Author.

   b. U.S. Department of Education. (2008). *Teaching children with attention deficit hyperactivity disorder: Instructional strategies and practices, 2008*. Washington, DC: U.S. Department of Education.

2. The student has quoted from an advertisement for the medication Concerta, which appears on pages 121-123 of the February 2009 issue of *O: The Oprah Magazine*. The volume number is 10 and the issue number is 2. The magazine is paginated by issue.

   a. Concerta [Medication]. (2009, February). *O: The Oprah Magazine, 10*(2), 121-123.

   b. Concerta [Advertisement]. (2009, February). *O: The Oprah Magazine, 10*(2), 121-123.

3. The student has paraphrased an article by Paul Steinberg found on the Web site of *The New York Times* (http://nytimes.com/). The article title is "Attention Surplus? Re-examining a Disorder" and is dated March 7, 2006.

   a. Steinberg, P. (2006, March 7). Attention surplus? Re-examining a disorder. *The New York Times*. Retrieved from http://nytimes.com/

   b. Steinberg, P. (2006, March 7). Attention surplus? Re-examining a disorder. *The New York Times*. Retrieved from *The New York Times* website.

Hacker/Sommers, *Working with Sources: Exercises for The Bedford Handbook*, 9th ed. (Boston: Bedford, 2014)

61-7 | APA documentation: reference list   **89**

4. The student has summarized material from an article in the journal *Developmental Psychology* titled "Gene x Environment Interactions in Reading Disability and Attention-Deficit/ Hyperactivity Disorder." The article is in volume 45, issue 1, published in January 2009, and is printed on pages 77-89. The journal is paginated continuously throughout the volume. The authors are Bruce F. Pennington, Lauren M. McGrath, Jenni Rosenberg, Holly Barnard, Shelley D. Smith, Erik G. Willcutt, Angela Friend, John C. DeFries, and Richard K. Olson.

   a. Pennington, B. F., et al. (2009). Gene x environment interactions in reading disability and attention-deficit/hyperactivity disorder. *Developmental Psychology, 45,* 77-89.

   b. Pennington, B. F., McGrath, L. M., Rosenberg, J., Barnard, H., Smith, S. D., Willcutt, E. G., . . . Olson, R. K. (2009). Gene x environment interactions in reading disability and attention-deficit /hyperactivity disorder. *Developmental Psychology, 45,* 77-89.

5. The student has summarized information from pages 26-28 of the book *Teaching Young Children with ADHD: Successful Strategies and Practical Interventions for PreK-3*, by Richard A. Lougy, Silvia L. DeRuvo, and David Rosenthal. The book was published in Thousand Oaks, California, in 2007 by Corwin Press.

   a. Lougy, R. A., DeRuvo, S. L., & Rosenthal, D. (2007). *Teaching young children with ADHD: Successful strategies and practical interventions for preK-3.* Thousand Oaks, CA: Corwin Press, 26-28.

   b. Lougy, R. A., DeRuvo, S. L., & Rosenthal, D. (2007). *Teaching young children with ADHD: Successful strategies and practical interventions for preK-3.* Thousand Oaks, CA: Corwin Press.

6. The student has quoted material from a journal article accessed in the Academic OneFile database. The journal is *American Journal of Psychology*, and the article, "Implicit Theories of Intelligence, Perceived Academic Competence, and School Achievement: Testing Alternative Models," was published in volume 119, issue 2, in 2006, on pages 223-238. The journal is paginated continuously throughout the volume. The article was written by Eleftheria Gonida, Grigories Kiosseoglou, and Angeliki Leondari. The article has no DOI (digital object identifier). The database's accession number for the document is A147872672, and the writer found the journal's Web site at http://www.press.uillinois.edu/journals/ajp.html.

   a. Gonida, E., Kiosseoglou, G., & Leondari, A. (2006). Implicit theories of intelligence, perceived academic competence, and school achievement: Testing alternative models. *American Journal of Psychology, 119,* 223-238. Retrieved from http://www.press .uillinois.edu/journals /ajp.html

   b. Gonida, E., Kiosseoglou, G., & Leondari, A. (2006). Implicit theories of intelligence, perceived academic competence, and school achievement: Testing alternative models. *American Journal of Psychology, 119,* 223-238. Retrieved from Academic OneFile database. (A147872672)

7. The student has paraphrased material from an article titled "The Role of Coping Humor in the Physical and Mental Health of Older Adults," published in November 2008 in the scholarly journal *Aging and Mental Health*, volume 12, issue 6, pages 713-718. The journal is paginated continuously through the volume. The article was written by Elsa Marziali, Lynn McDonald, and Peter Donahue.

    a.   Marziali, E., McDonald, L., & Donahue, P. (2008). The role of coping humor in the physical and mental health of older adults. *Aging and Mental Health, 12,* 713-718.

    b.   Marziali, E., McDonald, L., & Donahue, P. (2008, November). The role of coping humor in the physical and mental health of older adults. *Aging and Mental Health, 12,* 713-718.

8. The student summarized information from a podcast that was retrieved from the Web site http://www.pbs.org/merrow/podcast/. The podcast is called "The Right Answer?" from the series *Education Podcast with John Merrow.* It was produced by Jane Renaud, and there is no date of posting.

    a.   Renaud, J. (Producer). (n.d.). The right answer? [Audio podcast]. *Education podcast with John Merrow.* Retrieved from http://www.pbs.org/merrow/podcast/

    b.   Renaud, J. (Producer). (n.d.). The right answer? *Education podcast with John Merrow.* Retrieved from http://www.pbs.org/merrow/podcast/

9. The student has quoted from an online video file titled "How to Treat ADHD in Children," hosted by Matthew H. Erdelyi. No date is given for the video online; it was accessed by the student on January 30, 2009. The URL is http://www.articlesbase.com/videos/5min/29158215.

    a.   Erdelyi, M. H. (Host). (2009, 30 January). How to treat ADHD in children [Video file]. Retrieved from http://www.articlesbase.com/videos/5min/29158215

    b.   Erdelyi, M. H. (Host). (n.d.). How to treat ADHD in children [Video file]. Retrieved from http://www.articlesbase.com/videos/5min/29158215

10. The student has quoted material from an interview titled "What's New with ADHD?" The interview was conducted by Richard L. Peck and was published in volume 26, issue 1, of *Behavioral Health Management* in 2001. The interview was with E. Clarke Ross and appears on pages 26-30 of the journal. The journal is paginated by issue.

    a.   Peck, R. L. (2001). What's new with ADHD? [Interview with E. C. Ross]. *Behavioral Health Management, 26*(1), 26-30.

    b.   Ross, E. C. (2001). What's new with ADHD? [Interview by R. L. Peck]. *Behavioral Health Management, 26*(1), 26-30.

Hacker/Sommers, *Working with Sources: Exercises for The Bedford Handbook,* 9th ed. (Boston: Bedford, 2014)

61-7 | APA documentation: reference list   **91**

EXERCISE 61-8 ◆ APA documentation

To read about APA documentation, see 61 in *The Bedford Handbook*, Ninth Edition.

Write "true" if the statement is true or "false" if it is false.

1. A page number is required for all APA in-text citations.

2. In the text of a paper, the author(s) of a source and the source's date must be given either in a signal phrase introducing the cited material or in parentheses following it.

3. The list of references is organized alphabetically by authors' last names (or by title for a work with no author).

4. When citing a source with two authors in the text of the paper, use an ampersand (&) to join the names either in a signal phrase introducing the source or in parentheses at the end of the citation.

5. When you include a page number in parentheses at the end of a citation, precede the number with the abbreviation "p." or "pp."

6. APA style recommends using the present tense in a signal phrase introducing cited material (for example, "Baker reports that" or "Wu argues that").

7. When a paper cites two or more works by an author published in the same year, each work is assigned a lowercase letter, beginning with "a" and based on the alphabetical order of the works' titles. The letter appears after the year of publication in both in-text citations and the list of references.

8. If available, a date is supplied for all in-text citations; if no date is available, the abbreviation "n.d." is used instead.

9. If a work has eight or more authors, use the first author's name followed by "et al." in the reference list.

10. For a work with an unknown author, give the work's full title and its date in a signal phrase introducing the source or use a brief title and the date in parentheses following the source. Name "Anonymous" as the author only if the work specifies "Anonymous" as the author.

Hacker/Sommers, *Working with Sources: Exercises for The Bedford Handbook*, 9th ed. (Boston: Bedford, 2014)

EXERCISE 63-1 ◆ Thesis statements in *Chicago* papers

To read about thesis statements, see 63a in *The Bedford Handbook*, Ninth Edition.

Circle the letter of the sentence in each pair that would work well as the thesis statement for a research paper from five to ten pages long. Remember that a thesis should be a central idea that requires supporting evidence; it should be of adequate scope for a five-to-ten-page paper; and it should be sharply focused.

EXAMPLE

(a.) Although Jean Jacques Dessalines, commander of the revolutionary forces in Haiti, encouraged his soldiers to commit atrocities, his tactics may have been necessary to ensure that slavery would not return to Haiti.

b. After winning independence for Haiti and expelling people of European ancestry from the country, military leader Jean Jacques Dessalines declared himself emperor for life in 1804.

1. a. The development of general anesthesia made modern surgery possible, for it allowed surgeons to work slowly and carefully for the first time.

b. On October 16, 1846, observers of the first surgery performed on a person anesthetized with ether were astonished when the patient neither screamed nor seemed aware of any pain.

2. a. A surprising number of adventurers who achieved fame as explorers were later revealed to be charlatans who had not even found the places they said they had discovered.

b. Robert E. Peary is still credited by many people with the discovery of the North Pole in 1909, but the available evidence strongly suggests that he never reached his goal.

3. a. Many old Hollywood films have disappeared forever as the single surviving copies disintegrate from exposure to heat and moisture.

b. Because old Hollywood films capture historical moments that would otherwise be lost, restoring and preserving at least one copy of every possible film is a task that American scholars should support.

4. a. The electoral college, which was created in the eighteenth century to solve the problem of voters' lack of knowledge about candidates from other states, never worked as the framers of the Constitution intended.

b. The electoral college system was developed in the eighteenth century under circumstances much different from those facing the country today.

5. a. The United States caused needless civilian casualties by dropping an atomic bomb on Nagasaki in 1945, for the bombing of Hiroshima had already convinced the Japanese authorities to surrender.

b. Nagasaki, a populous Japanese city on an inlet of the East China Sea, was devastated on August 9, 1945, by the second atomic bomb dropped by the United States.

Hacker/Sommers, *Working with Sources: Exercises for The Bedford Handbook*, 9th ed. (Boston: Bedford, 2014)

63-1 | Thesis statements in *Chicago* papers **93**

6.   a.   Evidence from the trial of Bridget Bishop, the first woman hanged for practicing witchcraft in Salem, Massachusetts, indicates that Bishop had indeed been attempting to cast spells.

     b.   For centuries in much of Europe, women who were midwives or herbalists were often charged with practicing magic because they were regarded with deep suspicion by Christian clergymen.

7.   a.   The British, who are famous for their love of horses, used horses in warfare even when modern equipment, such as tanks, became an available option.

     b.   The extended carnage in the trenches of the western front in World War I could have been ended much sooner if British military officers had been willing to use tanks instead of horses in battle.

8.   a.   Israel has been struggling against one enemy or another since the United Nations voted to establish the Jewish state in 1948.

     b.   Citizens of Arab countries have long been encouraged to express grievances against Israel, while they are seldom permitted to speak out against oppressive policies of their own governments; this deflected anger has contributed to the vehemence of anti-Israeli feeling in many Arab lands.

9.   a.   To the surprise of modern scholars, the ancient Greek explanation for the prophetic powers of the oracle at Delphi—fumes that rose from the floor of the Temple of Apollo—may have a basis in fact, for the temple sits above the intersection of two underground faults that allow fumes of the hallucinogen ethylene to percolate up through the underlying limestone.

     b.   For more than twelve centuries, ancient Greeks traveled to the Temple of Apollo at Delphi to consult the oracle there, and they believed that the prophecies she made while in a trance were divinely inspired.

10.   a.   For decades, great buildings have been demolished in this country—from coast to coast and in cities and towns—because Americans have little sense of history.

     b.   The demolition of New York's Penn Station was the catalyst for the creation of the New York City Landmarks Preservation Commission, which helped save and restore other landmarks, including Grand Central Station and the New York Public Library.

Hacker/Sommers, *Working with Sources: Exercises for The Bedford Handbook*, 9th ed. (Boston: Bedford, 2014)

EXERCISE 63-2 ◆ Thesis statements in *Chicago* papers

To read about thesis statements, see 63a in *The Bedford Handbook*, Ninth Edition.

Circle the letter of the sentence in each pair that would work well as the thesis statement for a research paper from five to ten pages long. Remember that a thesis should be a central idea that requires supporting evidence; it should be of adequate scope for a five-to-ten-page paper; and it should be sharply focused.

EXAMPLE

a. Mohandas Gandhi was the leader of the Indian movement for independence from Britain.

(b.) Mohandas Gandhi was a successful political leader in large part because of his commitment to nonviolence during India's struggle for independence.

1. a. Ever since President John F. Kennedy was shot to death in November 1963, people have wondered whether his assassin, Lee Harvey Oswald, was working alone or as part of a conspiracy.

   b. The tragic circumstances surrounding President John F. Kennedy's death in 1963 were instrumental in allowing Lyndon B. Johnson to achieve many of his Great Society initiatives.

2. a. Lord Elgin removed friezes from the Parthenon and housed them in the British Museum in the early nineteenth century, thus earning them the name "Elgin marbles."

   b. The British Museum should honor Greece's request to have the ancient Parthenon friezes, known as the Elgin marbles, returned to their native country and displayed in a Greek museum.

3. a. Richard Nixon was probably not the first president to engage in illegal activity while in office, but Americans in 1973, war-weary and distrustful of authority, would no longer tolerate excuses based on historical precedent.

   b. Throughout history, presidents have been suspected of engaging in illegal activity, but few have been involved in scandals that caught the attention of the public, and even fewer have been impeached.

4. a. In the decades following World War II, many Americans began to realize the extent of the Japanese internment in the early 1940s.

   b. In the second half of the twentieth century, Americans were able to accept responsibility for the mistakes made during the Japanese internment of World War II largely because Japan was no longer seen as a military threat.

5. a. The most successful Jesuit missionaries in China during the Ming dynasty were able to adapt to Chinese culture: learning Mandarin, adopting Chinese clothing, and finding parallels between Christianity and the teachings of Confucius.

   b. Throughout history, the most successful missionaries have been those willing to engage in diplomacy with the people of power, respect the customs and language of the people they served, and emphasize similarities rather than differences between traditions.

Hacker/Sommers, *Working with Sources: Exercises for The Bedford Handbook*, 9th ed. (Boston: Bedford, 2014)

63-2 | Thesis statements in *Chicago* papers   **95**

6. a. Within two decades of their arrival in Peru, the Spanish nuns founded a convent in Cuzco called Santa Clara, which was given control over much of the confiscated Inca lands.

    b. Much of the economic power in colonial Peru was held by cloistered nuns, who played a crucial role in that country's early development.

7. a. In 1921, the long-term goal of the Chinese Communist Party was to form a Communist society, but it first focused on organizing the working class and on removing foreign influence from the government.

    b. Although not all historians agree, evidence suggests that the success of the Chinese Communist Party was due in large part to the Japanese invasions of Manchuria and central China in the 1930s.

8. a. Concern about a growing threat from Nazi Germany was the principal reason that the United States did not adequately prepare for a possible Japanese attack on Pearl Harbor.

    b. There is no way of knowing why the United States was so unprepared for the surprise Japanese attack on Pearl Harbor on December 7, 1941.

9. a. The United Nations had to weigh many competing agendas when it created the Jewish state of Israel in 1948.

    b. The British withdrawal from Palestine in 1947 had more to do with Britain's economic and political motives at home than with its relations with other countries.

10. a. In May 1966, Protestant loyalists in Northern Ireland formed the Ulster Volunteer Force, a paramilitary group whose aim was to combat the Irish Republican Army.

    b. Evidence suggests that protests in Northern Ireland against Catholic discrimination in the 1960s were heavily influenced by the American civil rights movement.

Hacker/Sommers, *Working with Sources: Exercises for The Bedford Handbook*, 9th ed. (Boston: Bedford, 2014)

EXERCISE 63-3 ◆ Avoiding plagiarism in *Chicago* papers

To read about avoiding plagiarism, see 63b in *The Bedford Handbook*, Ninth Edition.

Read the following passage and the information about its source. Then decide whether each student sample is plagiarized or uses the source correctly. If the student sample is plagiarized, write "plagiarized"; if the sample is acceptable, write "OK."

ORIGINAL SOURCE

> Unaccountable power always breeds resentment, especially when it is money power. The Rothschilds were demonized in Europe in much the same way as J. P. Morgan was in the United States—only more so, because they were Jewish. The myth of their omnipotence, in which they themselves sometimes believed, bred a virulent anti-Semitism, which fastened onto a uniquely visible Jewish family. To conservatives the Rothschilds were a standing threat to the established hierarchy; to socialists they stood for unbridled exploitation of the worker. Long after their power had disappeared, Hitler combined the two strands into a lethal cocktail, when he referred to the "rapacity of a Rothschild, who financed war and revolutions and brought the peoples into interest-servitude through loans." The origins of Auschwitz can be traced in part to this fateful coupling.

> From Skidelsky, Robert. "Family Values." Review of *The House of Rothschild: The World's Banker, 1849-1999* and *The House of Rothschild: Money's Prophets, 1789-1848*, both by Niall Ferguson. *New York Review of Books*, December 16, 1999, 24-29. [The source passage is from page 24.]

1. According to Robert Skidelsky, members of the Rothschild family were demonized in Europe much as J. P. Morgan was in the United States—only more so due to the fact that they were Jewish.[1]

2. Historian Robert Skidelsky notes, "The Rothschilds were demonized in Europe in much the same way as J. P. Morgan was in the United States—only more so, because they were Jewish."[2]

3. Robert Skidelsky observes that the Rothschild family earned particular enmity not only for being tremendously wealthy and powerful but also for being Jewish.[3]

4. Robert Skidelsky says of the Rothschilds that the myth of their omnipotence bred a virulent anti-Semitism, which fastened onto a uniquely visible Jewish family.[4]

5. To conservatives the Rothschilds were a standing threat to the established hierarchy; to socialists they stood for unbridled exploitation of the worker.

6. After the Rothschild family no longer wielded power, Robert Skidelsky writes, Hitler used both conservatives' and socialists' negative views of that wealthy family to incite hatred of the Jews.[5]

7. In the view of Robert Skidelsky, Hitler used both conservatives' and socialists' negative opinions of the wealthy Rothschild family and the power they had once wielded to incite hatred of the Jews.[6]

8. Robert Skidelsky points out the Rothschild family's place in Hitler's demonization of the Jews, noting that Hitler combined the two strands of the conservatives' and socialists' hatred of the Rothschilds into a lethal cocktail.

Hacker/Sommers, *Working with Sources: Exercises for The Bedford Handbook*, 9th ed. (Boston: Bedford, 2014)

63-3 | Avoiding plagiarism in *Chicago* papers **97**

9. Robert Skidelsky points out the Rothschild family's place in Hitler's demonization of the Jews, noting that Hitler "combined the two strands" of the conservatives' and the socialists' hatred of the Rothschilds to incite anti-Semitism.[7]

10. According to Robert Skidelsky, the beginnings of the concentration camps can be seen in part in the momentous combination of the conservatives' and the socialists' hatred of the Rothschilds.[8]

Hacker/Sommers, *Working with Sources: Exercises for The Bedford Handbook*, 9th ed. (Boston: Bedford, 2014)

EXERCISE 63-4 ◆ Avoiding plagiarism in *Chicago* papers

To read about avoiding plagiarism, see 63b in *The Bedford Handbook*, Ninth Edition.

Read the following passage and the information about its source. Then decide whether each student sample is plagiarized or uses the source correctly. If the student sample is plagiarized, write "plagiarized"; if the sample is acceptable, write "OK."

ORIGINAL SOURCE

    Years after the battle [Battle of the Little Bighorn] a number of Indians claimed that the soldiers became so terrified they dropped their guns. In fact, quite a few did drop their guns or throw them aside, although not necessarily in panic. The guns occasionally jammed because the soft copper shells—unlike hard brass—could be deformed by exploding powder, causing them to stick in the breech. Furthermore, troopers often carried loose ammunition in saddlebags where it was easily damaged. Another possible reason turned up when one of [Major] Reno's men talked with an ordnance officer. This officer subsequently wrote to the Chief of Ordnance that Custer's troops used ammunition belts made from scrap leather. The copper shells "thus had become covered with a coating of verdigris and extraneous matter, which had made it difficult to even put them in the chamber before the gun had been discharged at all. Upon discharge the verdigris and extraneous matter formed a cement which held the sides of the cartridge in place against the action of the ejector. . . ."

    Whatever the cause, it could take some time to pry a deformed shell out of the breech, or one that had been cemented in place, which explains why troopers under attack occasionally threw aside their rifles. To the Indians it must have appeared that a soldier who did this was terrified—as of course he might have been—but at the same time he might have been enraged.

From Connell, Evan S. *Son of the Morning Star: Custer and the Little Bighorn.* San
    Francisco: North Point Press, 1984. [The source passage is from pages 306-7.]

1. Evan S. Connell admits that many soldiers at the Battle of the Little Bighorn "did drop their guns or throw them aside" but argues that they did so "not necessarily in panic."[1]

2. According to Evan S. Connell, a number of Indians claimed that the soldiers at the Battle of the Little Bighorn were so frightened they dropped their weapons.[2]

3. As Evan S. Connell notes, the soldiers' guns at the Battle of the Little Bighorn might have jammed because the soft copper shells could be deformed by exploding powder, causing them to stick in the breech.[3]

4. Accepting the testimony that some soldiers at the Battle of the Little Bighorn abandoned their weapons, Evan S. Connell explains that the bullets had a disastrous tendency to stick in the soldiers' guns.[4]

5. Evan S. Connell points out that the weapons occasionally failed to fire because the pliant copper bullets—as opposed to hard brass—had been bent out of shape by detonating gunpowder, making them jam in the breech; in addition, loose ammunition was often toted in saddlebags where it was easily deformed.[5]

Hacker/Sommers, *Working with Sources: Exercises for*
The Bedford Handbook, 9th ed. (Boston: Bedford, 2014)

63-4 | Avoiding plagiarism in *Chicago* papers   **99**

6. Imagining Custer's men struggling to pry bullets out of their jammed guns in the heat of the Battle of the Little Bighorn, Evan S. Connell convincingly argues that while the soldiers might indeed have been frenzied with fear, those who decided to abandon their weapons probably did not act out of irrational panic.[6]

7. Evan S. Connell explains that in a letter to the Chief of Ordnance, an officer reported that Custer's troops used ammunition belts made from scrap leather and suggested that residue from the leather could have caused some shells to jam.[7]

8. An officer under the command of Reno reported that the soldiers' leather ammunition belts coated the shells with a substance that sometimes made the guns jam, according to Evan S. Connell.[8]

9. When the guns jammed, Evan S. Connell notes, it could take some time to pry a deformed shell out of the breech, or one that had been cemented in place, which explains why troopers under attack occasionally threw aside their rifles.

10. "To the Indians," Evan S. Connell writes, "it must have appeared that a soldier who [threw aside his rifle] was terrified—as of course he might have been—but at the same time he might have been enraged."[9]

Hacker/Sommers, *Working with Sources: Exercises for The Bedford Handbook*, 9th ed. (Boston: Bedford, 2014)

EXERCISE 63-5 ◆ Avoiding plagiarism in *Chicago* papers

To read about avoiding plagiarism, see 63b in *The Bedford Handbook,* Ninth Edition.

Read the following passage and the information about its source. Then decide whether each student sample is plagiarized or uses the source correctly. If the student sample is plagiarized, write "plagiarized"; if the sample is acceptable, write "OK."

ORIGINAL SOURCE

From the beginning, Nome [a city in Alaska] depended on its dogs. Teams were drafted into service as mail trucks, ambulances, freight trains, and long-distance taxis. The demand for sled dogs was so high, particularly during the northern gold rushes, that the supply of dogs ran out and a black market for the animals sprang up in the states. Any dog that looked as if it could pull a sled or carry a saddlebag—whether or not it was suited to withstand the cold—was kidnapped and sold in the north. "It was said at the time that no dog larger than a spaniel was considered safe on the streets" of West Coast port towns, said one sled dog historian.

From Salisbury, Gay, and Laney Salisbury. *The Cruelest Miles: The Heroic Story of Dogs and Men in a Race against an Epidemic.* New York: Norton, 2003. [The source passage is from page 20.]

1. According to Salisbury and Salisbury, so many people in Alaska wanted sled dogs during the gold rush period that large dogs were stolen from the United States and sold illegally in Alaska.[1]

2. Salisbury and Salisbury explain that the city of Nome, Alaska, depended on its dogs from the beginning of its existence.[2]

3. In Nome, as Salisbury and Salisbury point out, dogsleds acted as freight trains, mail trucks, taxis, and ambulances.[3]

4. Salisbury and Salisbury note that in Alaska during the gold rush, there were so many uses for sled dogs "that the supply of dogs ran out and a black market for the animals sprang up in the states."[4]

5. Every canine that appeared able to haul a dogsled or bear a pack on its back, notwithstanding its ability to deal with winter weather, was taken secretly and marketed in Alaska, say Salisbury and Salisbury.[5]

Hacker/Sommers, *Working with Sources: Exercises for The Bedford Handbook,* 9th ed. (Boston: Bedford, 2014)

63-5 | Avoiding plagiarism in *Chicago* papers   **101**

EXERCISE 63-6 ◆ Avoiding plagiarism in *Chicago* papers

To read about avoiding plagiarism, see 63b in *The Bedford Handbook*, Ninth Edition.

Read the following passage and the information about its source. Then decide whether each student sample is plagiarized or uses the source correctly. If the student sample is plagiarized, write "plagiarized"; if the sample is acceptable, write "OK."

ORIGINAL SOURCE

When Claudius died in October 54, at the age of sixty-three, there were several divergent accounts of what had caused his death. But according to the version which subsequently prevailed most widely, [his wife] Agrippina had killed him with poisoned mushrooms. This must be regarded as likely though not quite certain, since accidental loss of life frequently occurs in Italy owing to confusions between the harmless mushroom *boletus edulis* and the fatal *amanita phalloides*. Besides Agrippina had cleared the ground adequately for [her son] Nero's succession, and only had to wait. But perhaps that was just what she dared not do, because if Nero, who was nearly seventeen, did not come to the throne fairly soon, he might no longer be young enough to need her as his effective regent.

From Grant, Michael. *The Twelve Caesars.* New York: Scribner's, 1975. [The source passage is from page 147.]

1. The most likely but not quite certain cause of Claudius's death, says Grant, was that his wife had killed him with poisoned mushrooms.[1]

2. To bolster the view that Claudius might have eaten poisoned mushrooms accidentally, Grant notes that many people in Italy still die when they mistake an edible mushroom for a similar-looking but deadly one.[2]

3. According to Grant, there was no single predominant story but rather "several divergent accounts" of how Claudius died.[3]

4. Grant argues that Agrippina had prepared the way successfully for her son's eventual succession and needed only to bide her time until Nero would be emperor, with her acting as regent.[4]

5. Grant speculates that Agrippina could not wait for Claudius to die naturally because her son, Claudius's successor, would soon be old enough to rule on his own and would not need his mother as regent.[5]

Hacker/Sommers, *Working with Sources: Exercises for The Bedford Handbook*, 9th ed. (Boston: Bedford, 2014)

EXERCISE 63-7 ◆ Recognizing common knowledge in *Chicago* papers

To read about what constitutes common knowledge in history and other humanities, see 63b in *The Bedford Handbook*, Ninth Edition.

Read the student passage and determine whether the student needs to cite the source of the information in a *Chicago* paper. If the material does not need citation because it is common knowledge, write "common knowledge." If the material is not common knowledge and the student should cite the source, write "needs citation."

EXAMPLE

Small's Paradise, one of the most famous nightclubs of the Harlem Renaissance, was the only well-known New York nightclub of the era owned by an African American. **Needs citation** [This very specific fact about a little-known establishment requires citation. In addition, the statement that the nightclub was the *only* one owned by an African American must be supported by a source.]

1. In Rwanda in 1994, a civil war left hundreds of thousands of Tutsis and moderate Hutus dead.

2. Tong wars erupted in New York's Chinatown in the early decades of the twentieth century, giving that neighborhood the city's highest murder rate.

3. Abraham Lincoln was assassinated in Ford's Theatre in Washington, DC, as he sat watching a play.

4. After the Civil War, forty thousand former slaves had successful farms on the Sea Islands of South Carolina—the only place in the South where African Americans owned sizable quantities of land.

5. The eruption of a volcano on the island of Krakatau in Indonesia in 1883 spewed dense volcanic dust high into the atmosphere, blocking sunlight and lowering temperatures worldwide for months.

6. The US invasion of Cambodia in 1970 led to antiwar protests on many college campuses.

7. A Sherpa named Tenzing Norgay helped guide Edmund Hillary to the top of Mount Everest in 1953.

8. General George Custer and all of his men were killed at the Battle of the Little Bighorn.

9. The underground railroad provided shelter, guides, and assistance to runaway slaves as they made their way north to freedom.

10. Beginning in March 1988 and continuing for seventeen months, Saddam Hussein had his air force drop poison gas on more than two hundred Kurdish villages and towns in Iraq.

Hacker/Sommers, *Working with Sources: Exercises for The Bedford Handbook*, 9th ed. (Boston: Bedford, 2014)

63-7 | Recognizing common knowledge in *Chicago* papers **103**

EXERCISE 63-8 ◆ Integrating sources in *Chicago* papers

To read about integrating sources, see 63c in *The Bedford Handbook*, Ninth Edition.

Read the following passage and the information about its source. Then decide whether each student sample uses the source correctly. If the student has made an error in using the source, revise the sample to avoid the error. If the student has quoted correctly, write "OK."

ORIGINAL SOURCE

Practices associated with normal births in medieval Europe are shrouded in secrecy, not because the births were hidden at the time, but because they were a woman's ritual and women did not pass on information about them in writing. Indeed, we can be quite sure that the event of a birth was well known within the immediate community. Living close together, the neighbors would hear the cries of a woman in labor and would observe the midwife and female friends gathering around. But what occurred in the birthing chamber was not known to the men listening outside, and so it was not recorded. The learned clerical treatises on gynecology contain no descriptions of normal births, only abnormal ones. Male doctors never attended a normal birth, so they knew nothing about them. They were called in only when surgery was needed.

From Hanawalt, Barbara A. *Growing Up in Medieval London.* Oxford: Oxford University Press, 1993. [The source passage is from page 42.]

1. Barbara Hanawalt observes that little is known about how women gave birth in medieval Europe "not because the births were hidden at the time, but because they were a woman's ritual and women did not pass on information about them in writing."[1]

2. According to Barbara Hanawalt, "Practices associated with normal births in medieval Europe were secret."[2]

3. Although women in the Middle Ages, like women throughout history, had children, little is known about procedures related to ordinary births. "Practices associated with normal births in medieval Europe are shrouded in secrecy, not because the births were hidden at the time, but because they were a woman's ritual and women did not pass on information about them in writing."[3]

4. Barbara Hanawalt points out that neighbors would certainly have known when a birth was imminent because they "would hear the cries of a woman in labor and would observe the midwife and female friends gathering around."[4]

5. Barbara Hanawalt notes that because "what occurred in the birthing chamber was not known to the men . . . it was not recorded."[5]

6. According to Barbara Hanawalt,

    "Practices associated with normal births in medieval Europe are shrouded in secrecy, not because the births were hidden at the time, but because they were a woman's ritual and women did not pass on information about them in writing. Indeed, we can be quite sure that the event of a birth was well known within the immediate community. Living close together, the neighbors would hear the cries of a woman in labor and would observe the midwife and

Hacker/Sommers, *Working with Sources: Exercises for The Bedford Handbook*, 9th ed. (Boston: Bedford, 2014)

63-8 | Integrating sources in *Chicago* papers **105**

female friends gathering around. But what occurred in the birthing chamber was not known to the men listening outside, and so it was not recorded."[6]

7. Little is known today about normal births in the Middle Ages. Barbara Hanawalt explains that births "were a woman's ritual and women did not pass on information about them in writing. But what occurred in the birthing chamber was not known to the men listening outside, and so it was not recorded."[7]

8. Barbara Hanawalt notes, "[Medieval] learned clerical treatises on gynecology contain no descriptions of normal births, only abnormal ones. Male doctors never attended a normal birth, so they knew nothing about them. They were called in only when surgery was needed."[8]

9. Only abnormal births are described in learned medieval writings. "Male doctors never attended a normal birth, so they knew nothing about them. They were called in only when surgery was needed."[9]

10. Barbara Hanawalt observes that historians know little about normal childbirths in medieval times because childbirths were witnessed only by women, "and women did not pass on information about them in writing."[10]

Hacker/Sommers, *Working with Sources: Exercises for The Bedford Handbook*, 9th ed. (Boston: Bedford, 2014)

EXERCISE 63-9 ◆ Integrating sources in *Chicago* papers

To read about integrating sources, see 63c in *The Bedford Handbook*, Ninth Edition.

Read the following passage and the information about its source. Then decide whether each student sample uses the source correctly. If the student has made an error in using the source, revise the sample to avoid the error. If the student has quoted correctly, write "OK."

ORIGINAL SOURCE

> Hezbollah, with bases in the Bekaa and in Beirut's southern suburbs, quickly became the most successful terrorist organization in modern history. It has served as a role model for terror groups around the world; Magnus Ranstorp, the director of the Centre for the Study of Terrorism and Political Violence, at the University of St. Andrews, in Scotland, says that Al Qaeda learned the value of choreographed violence from Hezbollah. The organization virtually invented the multipronged terror attack when, early on the morning of October 23, 1983, it synchronized the suicide bombings, in Beirut, of the United States Marine barracks and an apartment building housing a contingent of French peacekeepers. Those attacks occurred just twenty seconds apart; a third part of the plan, to destroy the compound of the Italian peacekeeping contingent, is said to have been jettisoned when the planners learned that the Italians were sleeping in tents, not in a high-rise building.

From Goldberg, Jeffrey. "In the Party of God." *New Yorker*, October 7, 2002, 180-95.
[The source passage is from pages 182-83.]

1. According to Jeffrey Goldberg, Hezbollah "quickly became the most successful terrorist group in modern history."[1]

2. According to Jeffrey Goldberg, Hezbollah, with bases in the Bekaa and in Beirut's southern suburbs, "quickly became the most successful terrorist organization in modern history."[2]

3. Unfortunately, terrorist organizations learn from one another. Jeffrey Goldberg observes, for example, that Hezbollah "has served as a role model for terror groups around the world."[3]

4. Hezbollah has been successful. "It has served as a role model for terror groups around the world."[4]

5. Hezbollah has been so successful that Jeffrey Goldberg calls it "a role model for terror groups around the world."[5]

6. Jeffrey Goldberg notes that Hezbollah "virtually invented the multipronged terror attack when . . . it synchronized the suicide bombings, in Beirut, of the United States Marine barracks and an apartment building housing a contingent of French peacekeepers."[6]

7. According to Jeffrey Goldberg,

   > "[Hezbollah] virtually invented the multipronged terror attack when . . . it synchronized the suicide bombings, in Beirut, of the United States Marine barracks and an apartment building housing a contingent of French peacekeepers. Those attacks occurred just twenty seconds apart; a third part of the plan, to destroy the compound of the Italian peacekeeping contingent, is said to have been jettisoned when the planners learned that the Italians were sleeping in tents, not in a high-rise building."[7]

Hacker/Sommers, *Working with Sources: Exercises for The Bedford Handbook*, 9th ed. (Boston: Bedford, 2014)

63-9 | Integrating sources in *Chicago* papers   **107**

8. Jeffrey Goldberg credits Hezbollah with "virtually invent[ing] the multipronged terror attack" by bombing the quarters of the US Marines and French peacekeepers "just twenty seconds apart."[8]

9. Hezbollah scrapped a plan to bomb a third location in Beirut in 1983, explains Jeffrey Goldberg, "when the planners learned that the intended victims were not sleeping in a high-rise building."[9]

10. Jeffrey Goldberg claims that Hezbollah abandoned a proposed attack in Beirut "when the planners learned that the Italians [their intended victims] were sleeping in tents, not in a high-rise building."[10]

Hacker/Sommers, *Working with Sources: Exercises for The Bedford Handbook*, 9th ed. (Boston: Bedford, 2014)

EXERCISE 63-10 ◆ Integrating sources in *Chicago* papers

To read about integrating sources, see 63c in *The Bedford Handbook*, Ninth Edition.

Read the following passage and the information about its source. Then decide whether each student sample uses the source correctly. If the student has made an error in using the source, revise the sample to avoid the error. If the student has quoted correctly, write "OK."

ORIGINAL SOURCE

> Conflicts such as the seven major Anglo-French wars fought between 1689 and 1815 were struggles of endurance. Victory therefore went to the Power—or better, since both Britain and France usually had allies, to the Great Power coalition—with the greater capacity to maintain credit and to keep on raising supplies. The mere fact that these were *coalition* wars increased their duration, since a belligerent whose resources were fading would look to a more powerful ally for loans and reinforcements in order to keep itself in the fight. Given such expensive and exhausting conflicts, what each side desperately required was—to use the old aphorism—"money, money, and yet more money."

> From Kennedy, Paul. *The Rise and Fall of the Great Powers: Economic Change and Military Conflict from 1500 to 2000.* New York: Random House, 1987. [The source passage is from page 76.]

1. Kennedy refers to the seven wars between Britain and France from 1689 to 1815 as "struggles of endurance."[1]

2. In the Anglo-French wars prior to 1815, "victory . . . went to the Power—or better, since both Britain and France usually had allies, to the Great Power coalition—with the greater capacity to maintain credit and to keep on raising supplies."[2]

3. Kennedy notes that in the wars between Britain and France before 1815, the key to victory was building a coalition of countries so that "a belligerent whose resources were fading could keep itself in the fight."[3]

4. A Yale historian claims that the Anglo-French wars lasted longer when the opponents were able to form economic coalitions with other states: "a belligerent whose resources were fading would look to a more powerful ally for loans and reinforcements in order to keep itself in the fight."[4]

5. The Anglo-French wars between 1689 and 1815 were, as Kennedy has pointed out, "such expensive and exhausting conflicts . . . [that] each side desperately required . . . 'money, money, and yet more money.'"[5]

EXERCISE 63-11 ◆ Integrating sources in *Chicago* papers

To read about integrating sources, see 63c in *The Bedford Handbook*, Ninth Edition.

Read the following passage and the information about its source. Then decide whether each student sample uses the source correctly. If the student has made an error in using the source, revise the sample to avoid the error. If the student has quoted correctly, write "OK."

ORIGINAL SOURCE

Winnie [Mandela] had played no part in [Nelson] Mandela's social life since they separated: "It was as if they did not exist for each other," said their daughter Zindzi. But she still caused political problems. After campaigning vigorously and successfully as an ANC [African National Congress] candidate at the election she had become a prominent Member of Parliament. Mandela unwisely appointed her Deputy Minister of Arts, but she soon became involved in financial scandals: shady diamond deals, a dubious tourist project for black Americans, and an antipoverty program which allowed her huge expenses. Mandela made no move until she became openly disloyal: she accused the ANC of being preoccupied with appeasing whites, and challenged them to show they were in power.

From Sampson, Anthony. *Mandela: The Authorized Biography.* New York: Knopf, 1999.
[The source passage is from page 491.]

1. After Nelson Mandela and his wife, Winnie, separated, "It was as if they did not exist for each other."[1]

2. Sampson argues that after the Mandelas separated, Winnie Mandela "still caused political problems" for her husband.[2]

3. Sampson explains that when Winnie Mandela served as deputy minister of arts, "she became openly disloyal and accused the ANC of being preoccupied with appeasing whites."[3]

4. According to Sampson, Nelson Mandela "made no move [in response to Winnie's actions] until she became openly disloyal."[4]

5. When Winnie Mandela was deputy minister of arts, she benefited financially from "shady diamond deals, a dubious tourist project for black Americans, and an antipoverty program which allowed her huge expenses," according to Sampson's biography of Nelson Mandela.[5]

Hacker/Sommers, *Working with Sources: Exercises for The Bedford Handbook,* 9th ed. (Boston: Bedford, 2014)

EXERCISE 63-12 ◆ *Chicago documentation: identifying elements of sources*

To read about how to handle the elements of sources in *Chicago* citations, see 63d in *The Bedford Handbook*, Ninth Edition.

Circle the letter of the correct answer for each question using information in the source provided.

SOURCE: AN ARTICLE IN A PERIODICAL

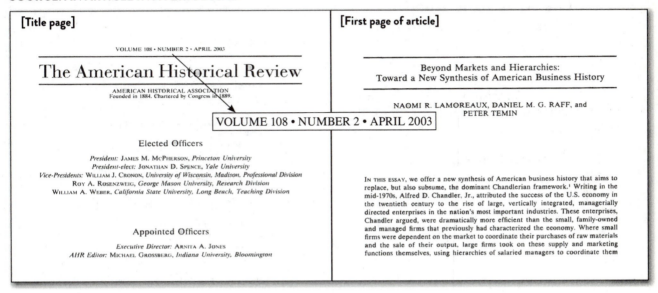

1. How would you begin a *Chicago*-style bibliography entry for this source?

   a. Lamoreaux, Naomi R., Daniel M. G. Raff, and Peter Temin. "Beyond Markets and Hierarchies: Toward a New Synthesis of American Business History."

   b. Lamoreaux, Naomi R., et al. "Beyond Markets and Hierarchies: Toward a New Synthesis of American Business History."

2. How would you cite the publication information for this article in a *Chicago*-style bibliography entry? The article begins on page 404 and ends on page 433.

   a. *American Historical Review* 108, no. 2 (2003): 404-33.

   b. *American Historical Review* 108.2 (2003): 404-33.

Hacker/Sommers, *Working with Sources: Exercises for
The Bedford Handbook*, 9th ed. (Boston: Bedford, 2014)

63-12 | *Chicago documentation: identifying elements of sources*   **111**

[Title page]

Black Athena

The Afroasiatic Roots
of Classical Civilization

VOLUME I
The Fabrication of Ancient Greece 1785–1985

Martin Bernal

Rutgers University Press
New Brunswick, New Jersey

[Copyright page]

First published in the United States by
Rutgers University Press, 1987
Fifth cloth and eighth paperback printing, April 1994
First published in Great Britain by
Free Association Books, 1987

© Martin Bernal 1987

Library of Congress Cataloging-in-Publication Data

Bernal, Martin
  Black Athena.
  (The fabrication of ancient Greece, 1785–1985; v. 1)
  Bibliography: p.
  Includes index.
  1. Greece—Civilization—Egyptian influences.
  2. Greece—Civilization—Phoenician influences.
  3. Greece—Civilization—To 146 B.C. I. Title.
  II. Title: Afroasiatic roots of classical civilization.
  III. Series: Bernal, Martin. Fabrication of ancient
  Greece, 1785–1985; v. 1.
  DF78.B398 1987   949.5   87–16408
  ISBN 0-8135-1276-X
  ISBN 0-8135-1277-8 (pbk.)

Manufactured in the United States of America
All rights reserved

The publication of *Black Athena* was aided by
the Hull Memorial Publication Fund
of Cornell University.

3. How would you prepare a *Chicago*-style bibliography entry for this source?

   a. Bernal, Martin. *Black Athena: The Afroasiatic Roots of Classical Civilization*. Vol. 1. New Brunswick, NJ: Rutgers University Press, 1987.

   b. Bernal, Martin. *The Fabrication of Ancient Greece 1785-1985*. Vol. 1 of *Black Athena: The Afroasiatic Roots of Classical Civilization*. New Brunswick, NJ: Rutgers University Press, 1987.

112   **63-12** | *Chicago* documentation: identifying elements of sources

Hacker/Sommers, *Working with Sources: Exercises for
The Bedford Handbook*, 9th ed. (Boston: Bedford, 2014)

SOURCE: AN ARTICLE FROM A DATABASE

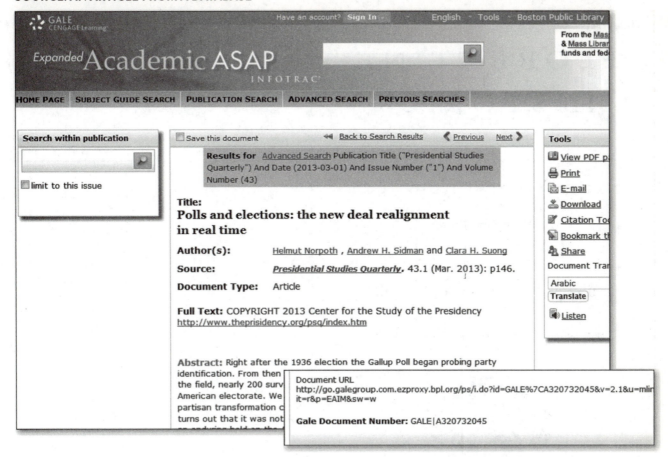

4. How would you cite the publication information for the periodical in this database record?

   a. *Presidential Studies Quarterly* 43, no. 1 (2013): 146+.

   b. *Presidential Studies Quarterly* 43 (March 2013): 146+.

5. What information would you place at the end of the entry, after the page number?

   a. Expanded Academic ASAP (A320732045)

   b. http://www.thepresidency.org/psq/index.htm

[Title page]

FLORENTINE HISTORIES

by

NICCOLÒ MACHIAVELLI

A New Translation by
LAURA F. BANFIELD
and
HARVEY C. MANSFIELD, JR.

With an Introduction by Harvey C. Mansfield, Jr.

PRINCETON UNIVERSITY PRESS
PRINCETON, NEW JERSEY

---

6. How would you begin a *Chicago*-style bibliography entry for this source?

a. Banfield, Laura F., and Harvey C. Mansfield Jr., trans. *Florentine Histories.*

b. Machiavelli, Niccolò. *Florentine Histories.* Translated by Laura F. Banfield and Harvey C. Mansfield Jr.

Hacker/Sommers, *Working with Sources: Exercises for The Bedford Handbook,* 9th ed. (Boston: Bedford, 2014)

7. How would you begin a *Chicago*-style bibliography entry for this source?

   a. Scammell, Michael. "The Russian Nobility under the Red Terror." Review of *Former People: The Final Days of the Russian Aristocracy*, by Douglas Smith.

   b. Smith, Douglas. *Former People: The Final Days of the Russian Aristocracy.*

8. How would you cite the publication information for this source in a *Chicago*-style bibliography entry? (Page references are not included because the source is not paginated online.)

   a. *New York Review of Books*, March 7, 2013. http://www.nybooks.com/articles/archives/2013/mar/07/russian-nobility-under-red-terror.

   b. *New York Review of Books*, 7 Mar. 2013. http://www.nybooks.com/articles/archives/2013/mar/07/russian-nobility-under-red-terror.

SOURCE: A SHORT DOCUMENT FROM A WEB SITE

[Home page]

[Internal page]

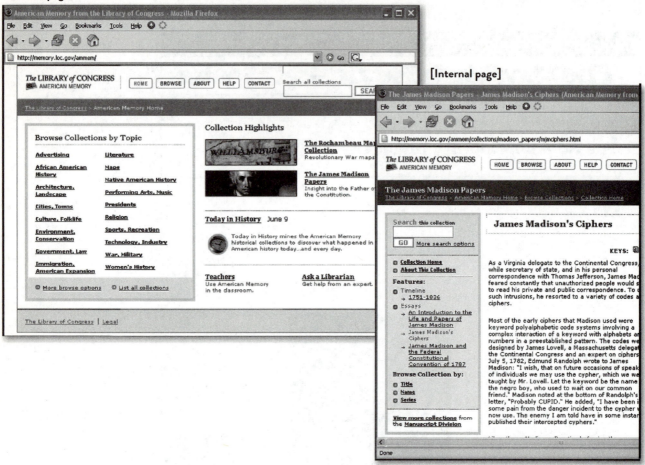

9. What would you cite as the sponsor of this source in a *Chicago*-style bibliography entry?

    a. Library of Congress

    b. No sponsor given

10. What is the correct *Chicago*-style bibliography entry for this source? (The site does not give an update date; the student accessed the site on April 3, 2013.)

    a. Library of Congress. "James Madison's Ciphers." American Memory. Accessed April 3, 2013. http://memory.loc.gov/ammem/collections/madison_papers/mjmciphers.html.

    b. "James Madison's Ciphers." American Memory. Library of Congress. Accessed April 3, 2013. http://memory.loc.gov/ammem/collections/madison_papers/mjmciphers.html.

Hacker/Sommers, *Working with Sources: Exercises for The Bedford Handbook*, 9th ed. (Boston: Bedford, 2014)

EXERCISE 63-13 ◆ *Chicago documentation: notes*

To read about how to use and format *Chicago*-style notes, see 63d in *The Bedford Handbook*, Ninth Edition.

Circle the letter of the *Chicago* note that is handled correctly.

EXAMPLE

The student has quoted from page 141 of *Cities Then and Now*, by Jim Antoniou; the book was published in New York in 1994 by Macmillan. This is the first reference to the book in the paper.

a.   1. Jim Antoniou, *Cities Then and Now* (New York: Macmillan, 1994), p. 141.

(b.)   1. Jim Antoniou, *Cities Then and Now* (New York: Macmillan, 1994), 141.

1.   The student has quoted from page 48 of the third edition of *The AIA Guide to New York City*, by Elliot Willensky and Norval White; the book was published in 1988 in San Diego by Harcourt Brace Jovanovich. This is the first reference to the source in this paper.

    a.   1. Elliot Willensky and Norval White, *The AIA Guide to New York City*, 3rd ed. (San Diego: Harcourt Brace Jovanovich, 1988), 48.

    b.   1. Willensky, Elliot, and Norval White, *The AIA Guide to New York City*, 3rd ed. (San Diego: Harcourt Brace Jovanovich, 1988), 48.

2.   The student has quoted from page 140 of *Cities Then and Now*, by Jim Antoniou; the book was published in New York in 1994 by Macmillan. This is the second reference to this source in the paper, and it does not immediately follow the first reference.

    a.   2. Jim Antoniou, *Cities Then and Now* (New York: Macmillan, 1994), 140.

    b.   2. Antoniou, *Cities Then and Now*, 140.

3.   The student has summarized information found on pages 16-17 of *Low Life*, by Luc Santé, a book published in New York by Farrar, Straus and Giroux in 1991. This is the second reference to the book in the paper, and it immediately follows the first reference.

    a.   3. Ibid., 16-17.

    b.   3. Santé, *Low Life*, 16-17.

4.   The student has quoted from page 7 of an article in the *Bridge*, volume 32, issue 1, published in 2002. The article, by Leslie E. Robertson, is titled "Reflections on the World Trade Center." This is the first reference to the article in the paper.

    a.   4. Leslie E. Robertson, "Reflections on the World Trade Center," *Bridge* 32, no. 1 (2002): 7.

    b.   4. Leslie E. Robertson. "Reflections on the World Trade Center." *Bridge* 32, no. 1 (2002): 7.

5.   The student has quoted from page 76 of "Building Plans," by Paul Goldberger. The article appeared in the weekly magazine the *New Yorker* on September 24, 2001. This is the first reference to the article in the paper.

    a.   5. Paul Goldberger, "Building Plans," *New Yorker*, September 2001, 76.

    b.   5. Paul Goldberger, "Building Plans," *New Yorker*, September 24, 2001, 76.

6. The student has quoted from page 78 of "Building Plans," by Paul Goldberger. The article appeared in the *New Yorker* on September 24, 2001. This is the second reference to the article in the paper, and it does not immediately follow the first reference.

   a.　　　6. Paul Goldberger ("Building Plans") 78.

   b.　　　6. Goldberger, "Building Plans," 78.

7. The student has quoted from page 14 of *Why Buildings Fall Down*, by Matthys Levy and Mario Salvadori, published in New York by W. W. Norton and Company in 1992. This is the second reference to the book in the paper, and it does not immediately follow the first reference.

   a.　　　7. Levy and Salvadori, *Why Buildings Fall Down*, 14.

   b.　　　7. Levy and others, *Why Buildings Fall Down*, 14.

8. The student has quoted from an interview with Brian Clark conducted by Matt Barrett. The interview, which appeared in an episode titled "Why the Towers Fell" on the television program *Nova*, was broadcast on April 30, 2002, on the Public Broadcasting System. The source is a broadcast interview, so there is no page number.

   a.　　　8. Matt Barrett, "Why the Towers Fell," *Nova*, PBS, April 2002.

   b.　　　8. Brian Clark, interview by Matt Barrett, "Why the Towers Fell," *Nova*, PBS, April 30, 2002.

9. The student has quoted from an article, "Wider Inquiry into Towers Is Proposed," by James Glanz. It appeared on May 2, 2002, in the online version of the *New York Times*. The URL is http://nytimes.com/2002/05/02/nyregion/02TOWE.html, and this is the first reference to the article in the paper.

   a.　　　9. James Glanz, "Wider Inquiry into Towers Is Proposed," *New York Times*, May 2, 2002, http://nytimes.com/2002/05/02/nyregion/02TOWE.html.

   b.　　　9. James Glanz, "Wider Inquiry into Towers Is Proposed," *New York Times*, May 2, 2002.

10. The student has summarized information from the article "Why Did the World Trade Center Collapse?" by Thomas W. Eagar and Christopher Musso. The article appeared in the online journal *JOM: The Journal of the Minerals, Metals, and Materials Society*, volume 53, issue 12, published in 2001. The URL of the article is http://www.tms.org/pubs/journals/JOM/0112/Eagar/Eagar-0112.html. This is the first reference to the article in the paper.

   a.　　　10. Thomas W. Eagar and Christopher Musso, "Why Did the World Trade Center Collapse?" *JOM: The Journal of the Minerals, Metals, and Materials Society*, http://www.tms.org/pubs/journals/JOM/0112/Eagar/Eagar-0112.html.

   b.　　　10. Thomas W. Eagar and Christopher Musso, "Why Did the World Trade Center Collapse?" *JOM: The Journal of the Minerals, Metals, and Materials Society* 53, no. 12 (2001), http://www.tms.org/pubs/journals/JOM/0112/Eagar/Eagar-0112.html.

EXERCISE 63-14 ◆ *Chicago* documentation: notes

To read about how to use and format *Chicago*-style notes, see 63d in *The Bedford Handbook*, Ninth Edition.

Circle the letter of the *Chicago* note that is handled correctly.

EXAMPLE

The writer is quoting from page 92 of *Chronicles of the Vikings: Records, Memorials, and Myths*, by R. I. Page; the book was published in Toronto in 1995 by University of Toronto Press. This is the first reference to the book in the paper.

a.   1. R. I. Page, *Chronicles of the Vikings: Records, Memorials, and Myths* (Toronto: University of Toronto Press, 1995), p. 92.

b.   1. R. I. Page, *Chronicles of the Vikings: Records, Memorials, and Myths* (Toronto: University of Toronto Press, 1995), 92.

1.   The student has quoted from page 7 of *Viking Age Iceland*, by Jesse L. Byock; the book was published in London in 2001 by Penguin Books. This is the first reference to the book in the paper.

   a.   1. Byock, Jesse L., *Viking Age Iceland* (London: Penguin Books, 2001), 7.

   b.   1. Jesse L. Byock, *Viking Age Iceland* (London: Penguin Books, 2001), 7.

2.   The student has quoted from page 92 of the book *Chronicles of the Vikings: Records, Memorials, and Myths*, by R. I. Page; the book was published in Toronto in 1995 by University of Toronto Press. This is the second reference to the book in the paper, and it does not immediately follow the first reference.

   a.   2. Page, *Chronicles of the Vikings*, 92.

   b.   2. R. I. Page, *Chronicles of the Vikings: Records, Memorials, and Myths* (Toronto: University of Toronto Press, 1995), 92.

3.   The writer has cited material from pages 271-72 of *An Introduction to Medieval Europe, 300-1500*, by James Westfall Thompson and Edgar Nathaniel Johnson; the book was published in New York by Norton in 1937. This is the second reference to the book in the paper, and it does not immediately follow the first reference.

   a.   3. Thompson and Johnson, *Introduction to Medieval Europe*, 271-72.

   b.   3. Thompson, *Introduction to Medieval Europe*, 271-72.

4.   The writer has summarized information found on page 132 of *Medieval Technology and Social Change*, by Lynn White Jr.; the book was published in London by Oxford University Press in 1962. This is the first reference to the book in the paper.

   a.   4. Lynn White Jr., *Medieval Technology and Social Change* (London: Oxford University Press, 1962), 132.

   b.   4. Lynn White Jr. *Medieval Technology and Social Change* (London: Oxford University Press, 1962). 132.

Hacker/Sommers, *Working with Sources: Exercises for The Bedford Handbook*, 9th ed. (Boston: Bedford, 2014)

63-14 | *Chicago* documentation: notes   **119**

5. The student has quoted from page 55 of the anonymous "Graenlendinga Saga." The work is found in *The Vinland Sagas: The Norse Discovery of America*, which was translated by Magnus Magnusson and Hermann Pálsson. Penguin Books published the book in London in 1965. This is the first reference to the book in the paper.

   a.   5. Anonymous, "Graenlendinga Saga," in *The Vinland Sagas: The Norse Discovery of America*, trans. Magnus Magnusson and Hermann Pálsson (London: Penguin Books, 1965), 55.

   b.   5. "Graenlendinga Saga," in *The Vinland Sagas: The Norse Discovery of America*, trans. Magnus Magnusson and Hermann Pálsson (London: Penguin Books, 1965), 55.

6. The student has quoted from "A Saga of Discovery," a short document found on the Web site Vikings Discovery and Landing at L'anse aux Meadows. There is no author, and the site is sponsored by Library and Archives Canada. The URL for the document is http://collections.ic .gc.ca/vikings/rediscovery1.htm, and this is the first reference to the document in the paper. The article does not have an update date; the student accessed it on September 23, 2002.

   a.   6. "A Saga of Discovery," Library and Archives Canada, accessed September 23, 2002, http://collections.ic.gc.ca/vikings/rediscovery1.htm.

   b.   6. "A Saga of Discovery," Vikings Discovery and Landing at L'anse aux Meadows, Library and Archives Canada, accessed September 23, 2002, http://collections.ic.gc.ca/vikings/rediscovery1 .htm.

7. The writer has quoted from page 109 of "Questions of Origin: Vikings, Vinland, and the Veracity of a Map," an article by Jessica Gorman in volume 162, issue 7, of the magazine *Science News*, published on August 17, 2002. This is the first reference to the article in the paper.

   a.   7. Jessica Gorman, "Questions of Origin: Vikings, Vinland, and the Veracity of a Map," *Science News*, August 17, 2002, 109.

   b.   7. Jessica Gorman, "Questions of Origin: Vikings, Vinland, and the Veracity of a Map," *Science News* 161, no. 7 (2002): 109.

8. The writer has quoted from page C1 of an article by John Noble Wilford, "Disputed Medieval Map Called Genuine After All." The article appeared in the *New York Times* on February 13, 1996. This is the first reference to the article in the paper.

   a.   8. John Noble Wilford, "Disputed Medieval Map Called Genuine After All," *New York Times*, February 13, 1996, C1.

   b.   8. John Noble Wilford, "Disputed Medieval Map Called Genuine After All," *New York Times*, February 13, 1996, sec. C.

9. The writer has quoted from John Noble Wilford's article "Disputed Medieval Map Called Genuine After All," which appeared on page C1 of the *New York Times* on February 13, 1996. This is the second reference to the article in the paper, and it immediately follows the first reference.

   a.   9. Wilford, "Disputed Medieval Map."

   b.   9. Ibid.

Hacker/Sommers, *Working with Sources: Exercises for The Bedford Handbook*, 9th ed. (Boston: Bedford, 2014)

10. The writer has quoted from a report by David Kestenbaum from August 5, 2002, titled "Is the Vinland Map a Fake?" The report is on the National Public Radio Web site, NPR, at http://www.npr.org/programs/morning/features/2002/aug/vinlandmap/index.html. This is the first reference to the source in the paper.

a.   10. David Kestenbaum, "Is the Vinland Map a Fake?," NPR, August 5, 2002, http://www.npr.org/programs/morning/features/2002/aug/vinlandmap/index.html.

b.   10. David Kestenbaum, "Is the Vinland Map a Fake?," NPR, National Public Radio, August 5, 2002, http://www.npr.org/programs/morning/features/2002/aug/vinlandmap/index.html.

EXERCISE 63-15 ◆ *Chicago* documentation: notes

To read about how to use and format *Chicago*-style notes, see 63d in *The Bedford Handbook*, Ninth Edition.

Circle the letter of the *Chicago* note that is handled correctly.

EXAMPLE

The student has quoted from page 111 of a book by Bill Gertz, *Breakdown: How America's Intelligence Failures Led to September 11*, published in Washington, DC, in 2002 by Regnery Publishing.

(a.)   1. Bill Gertz, *Breakdown: How America's Intelligence Failures Led to September 11* (Washington, DC: Regnery, 2002), 111.

b.   1. Gertz, Bill. *Breakdown: How America's Intelligence Failures Led to September 11*. Washington, DC: Regnery, 2002, 111.

1. The student has quoted from page 33 of a book by Victor Marchetti and John D. Marks, *The CIA and the Cult of Intelligence*, published in New York in 1974 by Dell Publishing Company.

    a.   1. Marchetti, Victor, and John D. Marks, *The CIA and the Cult of Intelligence* (New York: Dell, 1974), 33.

    b.   1. Victor Marchetti and John D. Marks, *The CIA and the Cult of Intelligence* (New York: Dell, 1974), 33.

2. The student has quoted from page 77 of an article, "The Stovepipe," by Seymour M. Hersh. It appeared in the *New Yorker* magazine on October 27, 2003.

    a.   2. Seymour M. Hersh, "The Stovepipe," *New Yorker*, Oct. 27, 2003, 77.

    b.   2. Seymour M. Hersh, "The Stovepipe," *New Yorker*, October 27, 2003, 77.

3. The student has paraphrased a passage from page A12 of a *New York Times* article, "Tenet Concedes Gaps in CIA Data on Iraq Weapons," by Douglas Jehl, which appeared on February 6, 2004. The article began on page A1 and continued on page A12.

    a.   3. Douglas Jehl, "Tenet Concedes Gaps in CIA Data on Iraq Weapons," *New York Times*, 6 February 2004, sec. A.

    b.   3. Douglas Jehl, "Tenet Concedes Gaps in CIA Data on Iraq Weapons," *New York Times*, February 6, 2004, sec. A.

4. The student has quoted from page 370 of an essay, "The Trouble with the CIA," by Thomas Powers, published in 2002 in the book *Intelligence Wars: American Secret History from Hitler to Al-Qaeda*. The book, a collection of Powers's essays, was published in New York by New York Review Books in 2002.

    a.   4. Thomas Powers, "The Trouble with the CIA," in *Intelligence Wars: American Secret History from Hitler to Al-Qaeda* (New York: New York Review Books, 2002), 370.

    b.   4. Thomas Powers, "The Trouble with the CIA," *Intelligence Wars: American Secret History from Hitler to Al-Qaeda* (New York: New York Review Books, 2002), 370.

5. The student has summarized an article, "CIA Intelligence Reports Seven Months before 9/11 Said Iraq Posed No Threat to US, Containment Was Working," by Jason Leopold. The article appeared on the Web site of the online magazine *Common Dreams* on February 17, 2004. The URL for the article is http://www.commondreams.org/views04/0217-12.htm.

    a.   5. Jason Leopold, "CIA Intelligence Reports Seven Months before 9/11 Said Iraq Posed No Threat to US, Containment Was Working," *Common Dreams*, February 17, 2004, http://www .commondreams.org/views04/0217-12.htm.

    b.   5. Jason Leopold, "CIA Intelligence Reports Seven Months before 9/11 Said Iraq Posed No Threat to US, Containment Was Working," *Common Dreams*, February 17, 2004, <http://www .commondreams.org/views04/0217-12.htm>.

6. The student has paraphrased material from the article "Why Can't Uncle Sam Spy?" by Anthony York. The article appeared in the online magazine *Salon* on September 18, 2001. The article's URL is http://archive.salon.com/news/feature/2001/09/18/spooks/index1.html.

    a.   6. Anthony York, "Why Can't Uncle Sam Spy?," September 18, 2001, *Salon*, http://archive .salon.com/news/feature/2001/09/18/spooks/index1.html.

    b.   6. Anthony York, "Why Can't Uncle Sam Spy?," *Salon*, September 18, 2001, http://archive .salon.com/news/feature/2001/09/18/spooks/index1.html.

7. The student has quoted from page 11 of an unsigned article, "Sincere Deceivers," published in the magazine the *Economist* on July 17, 2004.

    a.   7. "Sincere Deceivers," *Economist*, July 17, 2004, 11.

    b.   7. *Economist*, "Sincere Deceivers," July 17, 2004, 11.

8. The student has quoted from page 6 of a review of *The 9/11 Commission Report: Final Report of the National Commission on Terrorist Attacks upon the United States*, published by Norton in New York in 2004. The review, by Elizabeth Drew, was titled "Pinning the Blame" and was printed in the *New York Review of Books* on September 23, 2004.

    a.   8. Elizabeth Drew, "Pinning the Blame," review of *The 9/11 Commission Report: Final Report of the National Commission on Terrorist Attacks upon the United States*, *New York Review of Books*, September 23, 2004, 6.

    b.   8. Elizabeth Drew, "Pinning the Blame," review of *The 9/11 Commission Report: Final Report of the National Commission on Terrorist Attacks upon the United States* (New York: Norton, 2004), *New York Review of Books*, September 23, 2004, 6.

9. The student has quoted from page 14 of the article "In a Run-up to War, How Do We Report Intelligently on Intelligence?" written by Ted Gup in the March–April 2003 issue of *Columbia Journalism Review*. This is the second citation of the article in the paper. The first citation was in note 2.

    a.   9. Gup, 14.

    b.   9. Gup, "In a Run-up to War," 14.

124   **63-15** | *Chicago* documentation: notes

Hacker/Sommers, *Working with Sources: Exercises for The Bedford Handbook*, 9th ed. (Boston: Bedford, 2014)

10. The student has paraphrased a passage from page 81 of an article by Kenneth M. Pollack titled "Spies, Lies, and Weapons: What Went Wrong." The article appeared in the January-February 2004 issue of the *Atlantic*. This is the second citation of the article in the paper. The first citation was in note 9, citing page 80 of the article.

a.   10. Pollack, "Spies, Lies, and Weapons," 81.

b.   10. Ibid., 81.

Hacker/Sommers, *Working with Sources: Exercises for*
The Bedford Handbook, 9th ed. (Boston: Bedford, 2014)

63-15 | *Chicago* documentation: notes   **125**

EXERCISE 63-16 ◆ *Chicago* documentation: bibliography

To read about how to format a *Chicago*-style bibliography, see 63d in *The Bedford Handbook*, Ninth Edition.

Circle the letter of the *Chicago* bibliography entry that is handled correctly.

EXAMPLE

The student has quoted from a book, *Bad Land: An American Romance*, by Jonathan Raban. It was published in New York in 1996 by Pantheon Books.

a. Jonathan Raban. *Bad Land.* New York: Pantheon Books, 1996.

(b.) Raban, Jonathan. *Bad Land: An American Romance.* New York: Pantheon Books, 1996.

1. The student has paraphrased material from a book, *The Age of Reform: From Bryan to F.D.R.*, by Richard Hofstadter. It was published in 1955 in New York by Vintage Books.

   a. Richard Hofstadter. *The Age of Reform: From Bryan to F.D.R.* New York: Vintage Books, 1955.

   b. Hofstadter, Richard. *The Age of Reform: From Bryan to F.D.R.* New York: Vintage Books, 1955.

2. The student has cited the fifth edition of a book, *The American Promise: A History of the United States*, by James L. Roark, Michael P. Johnson, Patricia Cline Cohen, Sarah Stage, and Susan M. Hartmann. The book was published in Boston by Bedford/St. Martin's in 2012.

   a. Roark, James L., Michael P. Johnson, Patricia Cline Cohen, Sarah Stage, and Susan M. Hartmann. *The American Promise: A History of the United States.* 5th ed. Boston: Bedford/St. Martin's, 2012.

   b. Roark, James L., et al. *The American Promise: A History of the United States.* 5th ed. Boston: Bedford/St. Martin's, 2012.

3. The student has summarized material from an article, "America and Its Discontents," by Lilian and Oscar Handlin. The article appears on pages 15-37 of volume 64, issue 1, of the journal *American Scholar*, published in 1995.

   a. Handlin, Lilian and Oscar. "America and Its Discontents." *American Scholar* 64, no. 1: 15-37.

   b. Handlin, Lilian and Oscar. "America and Its Discontents." *American Scholar* 64, no. 1 (1995): 15-37.

4. The student has quoted from the article "Dust, the Thermostat: How Tiny Airborne Particles Manipulate Global Climate," by Sid Perkins, which appears on pages 200-202 of the September 29, 2001, edition of the magazine *Science News* (volume 160, issue 13).

   a. Perkins, Sid. "Dust, the Thermostat: How Tiny Airborne Particles Manipulate Global Climate." *Science News*, September 29, 2001, 200-202.

   b. Perkins, Sid. "Dust, the Thermostat: How Tiny Airborne Particles Manipulate Global Climate." *Science News*, September 29, 2001, 160 (13): 200-202.

Hacker/Sommers, *Working with Sources: Exercises for The Bedford Handbook*, 9th ed. (Boston: Bedford, 2014)

63-16 | *Chicago* documentation: bibliography **127**

5. The student has paraphrased material from an essay, "Learning from the Prairie," by Scott Russell Sanders. It appears on pages 3-15 of the anthology *The New Agrarianism: Land, Culture, and the Community of Life*, edited by Eric T. Freyfogle. The book was published in Washington, DC, in 2001 by Island Press.

   a. Sanders, Scott Russell. "Learning from the Prairie." In *The New Agrarianism: Land, Culture, and the Community of Life*, edited by Eric T. Freyfogle, 3-15. Washington, DC: Island Press, 2001.

   b. Sanders, Scott Russell. "Learning from the Prairie." In *The New Agrarianism: Land, Culture, and the Community of Life*. Ed. Eric T. Freyfogle, 3-15. Washington, DC: Island Press, 2001.

6. The student has cited an unpublished PhD dissertation, "The Righteous Cause: Some Religious Aspects of Kansas Populism," by Leland Levi Lengel. The dissertation was accepted in Eugene, Oregon, by the University of Oregon in 1968 and is listed in the ProQuest database with document number AAT 6900033.

   a. Lengel, Leland Levi. "The Righteous Cause: Some Religious Aspects of Kansas Populism." Unpublished PhD diss., University of Oregon, 1968. ProQuest (AAT 6900033).

   b. Lengel, Leland Levi. "The Righteous Cause: Some Religious Aspects of Kansas Populism." PhD diss., University of Oregon, 1968. ProQuest (AAT 6900033).

7. The student has quoted from an article, "Biography of Hugh Hammond Bennett," appearing on the Web site of the National Resources Conservation Service, a division of the US Department of Agriculture (the site's sponsor). The title of the site is National Resources Conservation Service. No author is listed for the article, and no date of posting is given. The date of access was February 29, 2004. The URL of the article is http://www.nrcs.usda.gov /about/history/bennett.html.

   a. "Biography of Hugh Hammond Bennett." National Resources Conservation Service. Accessed February 29, 2004. http://www.nrcs.usda.gov/about/history/bennett.html.

   b. "Biography of Hugh Hammond Bennett." National Resources Conservation Service. US Department of Agriculture. Accessed February 29, 2004. http://www.nrcs.usda.gov/about /history/bennett.html.

8. The student has cited a journal article accessed through a database. The article is "Small Farms, Externalities, and the Dust Bowl of the 1930s," by Zeynep K. Hansen and Gary D. Libecap. It appeared on pages 665-95 in the *Journal of Political Economy*, dated June 2004, volume 112, issue 3. The database is JSTOR, and the article is assigned the persistent URL http://www.jstor.org/stable/3555186.

   a. Hansen, Zeynep K., and Gary D. Libecap. "Small Farms, Externalities, and the Dust Bowl of the 1930s." *Journal of Political Economy* 112, no. 3 (2004): 665-95. http://www.jstor.org/stable /3555186.

   b. Hansen, Zeynep K., and Gary D. Libecap. "Small Farms, Externalities, and the Dust Bowl of the 1930s." *Journal of Political Economy* 112, no. 3 (2004): 665-95. JSTOR.

9. The student has cited an article, "Another One Bites the Dust," by Lester R. Brown, which appeared in an online publication, *Grist Magazine*, on May 29, 2001. The URL of the article is http://www.gristmagazine.com/maindish/brown052901.asp.

   a. Brown, Lester R. "Another One Bites the Dust." http://www.gristmagazine.com/maindish/brown052901.asp.

   b. Brown, Lester R. "Another One Bites the Dust." *Grist Magazine*, May 29, 2001. http://www.gristmagazine.com/maindish/brown052901.asp.

10. The student has quoted dialogue from the film *The Grapes of Wrath*, directed by John Ford. The film was produced in 1940 by Twentieth Century Fox. The student viewed a DVD released in 2004 by Fox Home Entertainment in Beverly Hills, California.

   a. Ford, John, dir. *The Grapes of Wrath*. 1940; Beverly Hills, CA: Fox Home Entertainment, 2004. DVD.

   b. *The Grapes of Wrath*. Directed by John Ford. 1940; Beverly Hills, CA: Fox Home Entertainment, 2004. DVD.

Hacker/Sommers, *Working with Sources: Exercises for*
The Bedford Handbook, 9th ed. (Boston: Bedford, 2014)

63-16 | *Chicago documentation: bibliography*   **129**

EXERCISE 63-17 ◆ *Chicago* documentation: bibliography

To read about how to format a *Chicago*-style bibliography, see 63d in *The Bedford Handbook*, Ninth Edition.

Circle the letter of the *Chicago* bibliography entry that is handled correctly.

EXAMPLE

The student has summarized information from a book titled *Pearl Harbor: Warning and Decision*, written by Roberta Wohlstetter and published in 1962 by Stanford University Press in Stanford, California.

a. Wohlstetter, Roberta. *Pearl Harbor: Warning and Decision* (Stanford: Stanford University Press, 1962).

b. Wohlstetter, Roberta. *Pearl Harbor: Warning and Decision.* Stanford: Stanford University Press, 1962.

1. The student has quoted from an article appearing on page A36 of the December 7, 2008, *New York Times* titled "Report Debunks Theory That the US Heard a Coded Warning about Pearl Harbor," by Sam Roberts.

   a. Roberts, Sam. "Report Debunks Theory That the US Heard a Coded Warning about Pearl Harbor." *New York Times*, December 7, 2008, A36.

   b. Roberts, Sam. "Report Debunks Theory That the US Heard a Coded Warning about Pearl Harbor." *New York Times*, December 7, 2008, sec. A.

2. The student has summarized material from an essay, "Pearl Harbor as an Intelligence Failure," written by David Kahn and printed on pages 158-96 of the book *Pearl Harbor and the Coming of the Pacific War: A Brief History with Documents and Essays*, edited by Akira Iriye. The book was published in Boston in 1999 by Bedford/St. Martin's and is part of a series called the Bedford Series in History and Culture.

   a. Kahn, David. "Pearl Harbor as an Intelligence Failure." In *Pearl Harbor and the Coming of the Pacific War: A Brief History with Documents and Essays*, edited by Akira Iriye, 158-96. Bedford Series in History and Culture. Boston: Bedford/St. Martin's, 1999.

   b. Iriye, Akira, ed. *Pearl Harbor and the Coming of the Pacific War: A Brief History with Documents and Essays.* "Pearl Harbor as an Intelligence Failure," by David Kahn, 158-96. Bedford Series in History and Culture. Boston: Bedford/St. Martin's, 1999.

3. The student has quoted material from an untitled review of the book *A Date Which Will Live: Pearl Harbor in American Memory*, by Emily S. Rosenberg. The book was published in 2003 in Durham, NC, by Duke University Press. The review was written by Naoko Shibusawa and appears on page 1519 of the *Journal of American History*, volume 91, issue 4, published in 2005.

   a. Rosenberg, Emily S. *A Date Which Will Live: Pearl Harbor in American Memory.* Reviewed by Naoko Shibusawa. *Journal of American History* 91, no. 4 (2005): 1519.

   b. Shibusawa, Naoko. Review of *A Date Which Will Live: Pearl Harbor in American Memory*, by Emily S. Rosenberg. *Journal of American History* 91, no. 4 (2005): 1519.

Hacker/Sommers, *Working with Sources: Exercises for The Bedford Handbook*, 9th ed. (Boston: Bedford, 2014)

63-17 | *Chicago* documentation: bibliography   **131**

4. The student has summarized information from an article appearing on pages 75-101 of the *Journal of Military History*, volume 58, issue 1, which was published in January 1994. The article is titled "Pinpointing Devastation: American Air Campaign Planning before Pearl Harbor" and was written by Mark Clodfelter.

   a. Clodfelter, Mark. "Pinpointing Devastation: American Air Campaign Planning before Pearl Harbor." *Journal of Military History* 58, no. 1: 75-101.

   b. Clodfelter, Mark. "Pinpointing Devastation: American Air Campaign Planning before Pearl Harbor." *Journal of Military History* 58, no. 1 (1994): 75-101.

5. The student has quoted material from a letter published on pages 184-87 of the book *War Letters: Extraordinary Correspondence from American Wars*, which was edited by Andrew Carroll. The letter was written by Paul E. Spangler on December 17, 1941, and was sent to Izee Reds. The book was published in New York by Scribner in 2001.

   a. Spangler, Paul E. Paul E. Spangler to Izee Reds, 17 December 1941. In *War Letters: Extraordinary Correspondence from American Wars*, edited by Andrew Carroll, 184-87. New York: Scribner, 2001.

   b. Spangler, Paul E. Paul E. Spangler to Izee Reds, December 17, 1941. In *War Letters: Extraordinary Correspondence from American Wars*, edited by Andrew Carroll, 184-87. New York: Scribner, 2001.

6. The student has paraphrased material from the short work "United States Naval Base, Pearl Harbor," on the Web site Aviation: From Sand Dunes to Sonic Booms. There is no named author and no update date. The site is sponsored by the National Park Service. The student accessed the material at http://www.nps.gov/nr/travel/aviation/prl.htm on December 3, 2008.

   a. "United States Naval Base, Pearl Harbor." Aviation: From Sand Dunes to Sonic Booms. National Park Service. Accessed December 3, 2008. http://www.nps.gov/nr/travel/aviation/prl.htm.

   b. "United States Naval Base, Pearl Harbor." Aviation: From Sand Dunes to Sonic Booms. http://www.nps.gov/nr/travel/aviation/prl.htm.

7. The student has paraphrased material from a posting to the H-war discussion list written by Christopher Koontz on January 22, 2009. The title of the posting is "Trivialization of History," and the URL is http://www.h-net.org/logsearch/?phrase=pearl+harbor&type=keyword&hitlimit=25&field=&nojg=on&smonth=00&syear=1989&emonth=11&eyear=2029&order=-@DPB.

   a. Koontz, Christopher. "Trivialization of History." Posting to the H-war discussion list. January 22, 2009. http://www.h-net.org/logsearch/?phrase=pearl+harbor&type=keyword&hitlimit=25&field=&nojg=on&smonth=00&syear=1989&emonth=11&eyear=2029&order=-@DPB.

   b. No entry; discussion list postings are not included in a CMS bibliography.

8. The student has summarized a few paragraphs from pages 648-53 of the biography *Franklin Delano Roosevelt: Champion of Freedom*, by Conrad Black. The book was published in New York by PublicAffairs in 2003.

    a. Black, Conrad. *Franklin Delano Roosevelt: Champion of Freedom*, 648-53. New York: PublicAffairs, 2003.

    b. Black, Conrad. *Franklin Delano Roosevelt: Champion of Freedom*. New York: PublicAffairs, 2003.

9. The student has quoted dialogue from the documentary movie *Pearl Harbor: Legacy of Attack*, which was narrated by Tom Brokaw. The student viewed the DVD version, released in 2001. The producer/distributor is National Geographic Video in Washington, DC.

    a. *Pearl Harbor: Legacy of Attack*. Narrated by Tom Brokaw. Washington, DC: National Geographic Video, 2001. DVD.

    b. *Pearl Harbor: Legacy of Attack*. Narrated by Tom Brokaw. Washington, DC: National Geographic Video, 2001.

10. The student has quoted from an article titled "Unlocking a Photograph's Secrets (Pearl Harbor Attack, 1941)." The article has no named author and appeared in *American History*, volume 30, issue 1, in April 1995 on page 74. The student found the article in the Expanded Academic ASAP database, where it was assigned the document number A16552901. The database does not give a DOI (digital object identifier).

    a. "Unlocking a Photograph's Secrets (Pearl Harbor Attack, 1941)." *American History* 30, no. 1 (1995): 74. Expanded Academic ASAP (A16552901).

    b. "Unlocking a Photograph's Secrets (Pearl Harbor Attack, 1941)." *American History* 30, no. 1 (1995): 74. Expanded Academic ASAP.

Hacker/Sommers, *Working with Sources: Exercises for The Bedford Handbook*, 9th ed. (Boston: Bedford, 2014)

63-17 | *Chicago* documentation: bibliography   **133**

EXERCISE 63-18 ◆ *Chicago* documentation: bibliography

To read about how to format a *Chicago*-style bibliography, see 63d in *The Bedford Handbook*, Ninth Edition.

Circle the letter of the *Chicago* bibliography entry that is handled correctly.

EXAMPLE

The student has summarized information from the book *A History of Modern Russia: From Nicholas II to Vladimir Putin*, by Robert Service. The book was published in 2005 by Harvard University Press in Cambridge, MA.

a. Robert Service. *A History of Modern Russia: From Nicholas II to Vladimir Putin*. Cambridge, MA: Harvard University Press, 2005.

(b.) Service, Robert. *A History of Modern Russia: From Nicholas II to Vladimir Putin*. Cambridge, MA: Harvard University Press, 2005.

1. The student has quoted material from the book *The Communist Manifesto*, by Karl Marx and Friedrich Engels. The book was originally published in 1888 and was released online by Project Gutenberg in 2005. The student accessed the book at http://www.gutenberg.org /etext/61. The original publisher is unknown.

   a. Marx, Karl, and Friedrich Engels. *The Communist Manifesto*. 1888. Project Gutenberg, 2005. http://www.gutenberg.org/etext/61.

   b. Marx, Karl, and Engels, Friedrich. *The Communist Manifesto*. 1888. Project Gutenberg, 2005. http://www.gutenberg.org/etext/61.

2. The student has summarized material from the article "Soviet and American Communist Parties" on the Web site Soviet Archives Exhibit. The article and the Web site do not have an author. The site is sponsored by the Library of Congress. The URL for the article is http://www.ibiblio.org/expo/soviet.exhibit/party.html, and the student accessed the site on January 13, 2009.

   a. Anonymous. "Soviet and American Communist Parties." Soviet Archives Exhibit. Library of Congress. Accessed January 13, 2009. http://www.ibiblio.org/expo/soviet.exhibit/party.html.

   b. "Soviet and American Communist Parties." Soviet Archives Exhibit. Library of Congress. Accessed January 13, 2009. http://www.ibiblio.org/expo/soviet.exhibit/party.html.

3. Near the beginning of the research paper, the student has summarized material from the book *Why Did the Soviet Union Collapse? Understanding Historical Change*, by Robert W. Strayer. The book was published by M. E. Sharpe in 1998 in Armonk, NY. Near the end of the paper, the student has summarized material from an article by Robert W. Strayer titled "Decolonization, Democratization, and Communist Reform: The Soviet Collapse in Comparative Perspective." The article appeared on pages 375-406 of *Journal of World History*, volume 12, issue 2, in 2001.

   a. Strayer, Robert W. "Decolonization, Democratization, and Communist Reform: The Soviet Collapse in Comparative Perspective." *Journal of World History* 12, no. 2 (2001): 375-406.

   ------. *Why Did the Soviet Union Collapse? Understanding Historical Change*. Armonk, NY: M. E. Sharpe, 1998.

Hacker/Sommers, *Working with Sources: Exercises for The Bedford Handbook*, 9th ed. (Boston: Bedford, 2014)

63-18 | *Chicago* documentation: bibliography **135**

b. Strayer, Robert W. *Why Did the Soviet Union Collapse? Understanding Historical Change.* Armonk, NY: M. E. Sharpe, 1998.

------. "Decolonization, Democratization, and Communist Reform: The Soviet Collapse in Comparative Perspective." *Journal of World History* 12, no. 2 (2001): 375-406.

4. The student has quoted from an e-mail message received from a relative, Max Pavlovsky, who lived in the Soviet Union during his childhood. The e-mail was sent to the student on December 28, 2008.

a. Pavlovsky, Max. E-mail message to the author. December 28, 2008.

b. No entry in the bibliography for e-mail messages

5. The student has quoted from the film *The Battleship Potemkin*, directed by Sergei Eisenstein in 1925. The student viewed a DVD that was distributed in 2004 by Delta Entertainment in Los Angeles.

a. *The Battleship Potemkin*. Directed by Sergei Eisenstein. Los Angeles: Delta Entertainment, 2004. DVD.

b. *The Battleship Potemkin*. Directed by Sergei Eisenstein. 1925; Los Angeles: Delta Entertainment, 2004. DVD.

6. The student has quoted material from page 202 of the book *The Rise of Russia and the Fall of the Soviet Empire*, by John B. Dunlop. The book was published in 1993 by Princeton University Press. The material being quoted originally appeared on page 64 in a September 2, 1991, *Newsweek* article by Henry A. Kissinger titled "Dealing with a New Russia."

a. Kissinger, Henry A. "Dealing with a New Russia." *Newsweek*, September 2, 1991, 64. Quoted in John B. Dunlop, *The Rise of Russia and the Fall of the Soviet Empire* (Princeton, NJ: Princeton University Press, 1993), 202.

b. Kissinger, Henry A. "Dealing with a New Russia." Quoted in John B. Dunlop, *The Rise of Russia and the Fall of the Soviet Empire* (Princeton, NJ: Princeton University Press, 1993), 202.

7. The student has paraphrased material from the article "Redesigning History in Contemporary Russia," by Catherine Merridale. The article appeared on pages 13-28 of the *Journal of Contemporary History*, volume 38, issue 1, which was published in 2003. The student accessed the article on February 16, 2009, from the JSTOR database, which assigns the article the stable URL http://www.jstor.org/stable/3180694.

a. Merridale, Catherine. "Redesigning History in Contemporary Russia." *Journal of Contemporary History* 38, no. 1 (2003): 13-28. http://www.jstor.org/stable/3180694.

b. Merridale, Catherine. "Redesigning History in Contemporary Russia." *Journal of Contemporary History*. http://www.jstor.org/stable/3180694.

Hacker/Sommers, *Working with Sources: Exercises for The Bedford Handbook*, 9th ed. (Boston: Bedford, 2014)

8. The student has summarized information from an article titled "Narrating the Russian Revolution: Institutionalism and Continuity across Regime Change," by Don K. Rowney. The article appeared on pages 79-105 of *Comparative Studies in Society and History*, volume 47, issue 1, published in 2005.

   a. Rowney, Don K. "Narrating the Russian Revolution: Institutionalism and Continuity across Regime Change." *Comparative Studies in Society and History* 47, no. 1 (2005): 79-105.

   b. Rowney, Don K. "Narrating the Russian Revolution: Institutionalism and Continuity across Regime Change." *Comparative Studies in Society and History* (2005): 79-105.

9. The student has paraphrased material from a newspaper article titled "Russians Get New, Fond Glimpse of the Last Czar," by Courtney Weaver. The article appeared on page 8 in section A of the July 20, 2008, *New York Times*.

   a. Weaver, Courtney. "Russians Get New, Fond Glimpse of the Last Czar." *New York Times*, July 20, 2008, sec. A, p. 8.

   b. Weaver, Courtney. "Russians Get New, Fond Glimpse of the Last Czar." *New York Times*, July 20, 2008, sec. A.

10. The student is quoting material from an article titled "Russia's Struggle with the Language of Marketing in the Communist and Post-Communist Eras," by Nigel Holden, Andrei Kuznetsov, and Jeryl Whitelock. The article appeared on pages 474-88 of *Business History*, volume 50, issue 4, published in 2008.

   a. Holden, Nigel, Andrei Kuznetsov, and Jeryl Whitelock. "Russia's Struggle with the Language of Marketing in the Communist and Post-Communist Eras." *Business History* 50, no. 4 (2008): 474-88.

   b. Holden, Nigel, et al. "Russia's Struggle with the Language of Marketing in the Communist and Post-Communist Eras." *Business History* 50, no. 4 (2008): 474-88.

EXERCISE 63-19 ◆ *Chicago documentation*

To read about *Chicago* documentation, see 63d in *The Bedford Handbook*, Ninth Edition.

Write "true" if the statement is true or "false" if it is false.

1. Each summary, paraphrase, and direct quotation from a source cited in the paper requires a footnote or an endnote.

2. The bibliography should include only works that are cited with notes in the text of the paper.

3. If a source has already been cited in the paper, no note is needed for further references to that source.

4. When a work is cited in two consecutive notes, the note for the second citation should include only the page number.

5. The bibliography is organized alphabetically by authors' (or editors') last names (or by title for a work with no author).

6. The note and bibliography entry for a source found on a Web site should include the URL in angle brackets.

7. A note should list the author's first name first; a bibliography entry should list the last name first.

8. Both the note and its corresponding bibliography entry should begin with a paragraph-style indent.

9. Notes may be given at the foot of a page or they may appear at the end of the paper, right before the bibliography.

10. Note numbers in the text of the paper appear in parentheses.

Hacker/Sommers, *Working with Sources: Exercises for*
The Bedford Handbook, 9th ed. (Boston: Bedford, 2014)

Answers to Exercises

EXERCISE 50-1 Research questions, page 1

1. b. This question, which raises issues of debate, is intellectually challenging. The other question, which calls for a definition, is merely factual.
2. b. This question is focused enough (dealing with a specific region and a specific environmental problem) to cover adequately in ten to fifteen pages.
3. a. This question is intellectually challenging: To answer it, the writer will need to weigh evidence and judge the soundness of competing arguments. The other question leads simply to fact searching.
4. a. This question is focused on a specific demographic in a specific country and can be covered adequately in ten to fifteen pages.
5. b. This question is grounded in evidence; to answer it, the writer would need to rely on more than just speculation.
6. a. This question is challenging; it requires the writer to analyze and interpret historical evidence. The other question leads simply to fact searching.
7. b. This question is focused on one approach to safe agriculture—government regulation—and can be covered adequately in ten to fifteen pages.
8. a. This question is intellectually challenging because it requires the writer to weigh evidence about a problem and its solution. The other question leads simply to fact searching.
9. b. A paper answering this question would be grounded in evidence and would require analysis of the effects on elementary education. The other question suggests that the writer will base the paper on moral beliefs.
10. b. This question is challenging because it leads to a causal analysis. The other question leads to a reporting of facts.

EXERCISE 53-1 Thesis statements in MLA papers, page 3

1. b. This sentence makes an assertion that can be developed in the paper. The other version merely states facts.
2. b. This sentence makes a clear and focused assertion that can be argued in the paper. The other version is too vague.
3. a. This sentence makes an assertion leading to a historical analysis.
4. a. This thesis limits itself to a narrow topic—stricter computer privacy rights—and it focuses on a way the government might restrict those rights. The other version is too broad and too vague.
5. b. This sentence focuses clearly on the benefits of online grocery shopping. The sentence also suggests an organizational plan for the paper.
6. b. This sentence makes a clear assertion and suggests an organizational plan for the paper.
7. b. This sentence restricts the topic to one idea that the writer can develop in depth. The other version is too broad.
8. b. This version focuses precisely on the points the writer will develop in the paper. The other version is too vague and broad.
9. b. This version focuses on an idea that the writer can develop in the paper.
10. a. This sentence makes an assertion that is restricted enough for the writer to develop in depth in the paper.

EXERCISE 53-2 Thesis statements in MLA papers, page 5

1. a. This statement asserts a position about the Fairness Doctrine that can be argued in a paper. The other statement is too factual to make an effective thesis.
2. a. This statement asserts a position and suggests a clear focus for a paper. The other statement is too broad and unfocused to make an effective thesis.
3. b. This statement makes a focused proposal that can be supported in a paper. The other statement makes a claim, but it is too broad and vague to work as a thesis for a paper.
4. b. This statement makes an assertion that can be argued with evidence in a paper. The other statement is too factual to make an effective thesis.
5. b. This statement makes a focused proposal, based on a fact, that can be argued in a paper. The other statement presents a fact, but it does not take a position on an issue, so it would not make an effective thesis.
6. a. This statement makes a claim that can be argued in a paper with evidence from the novel and other sources. The other statement is too factual and trivial to work as a thesis.
7. b. This statement provides a proposed course of action that can be supported with evidence in a paper. The other statement is vague; it lacks a focused claim that can be argued in a paper.
8. a. This statement makes a focused assertion that can be argued with evidence in a paper. The other statement is too vague to make an effective thesis.
9. a. This statement makes a claim that can be supported with evidence in a paper. The other statement is too factual to be an effective thesis.
10. b. This statement makes an assertion that sets up a framework for a paper. The other statement merely gives the publication dates of two books.

EXERCISE 54-1 Avoiding plagiarism in MLA papers, page 7

1. OK. This sentence is written in the student's own words, and it is correctly documented with an MLA in-text citation. The citation consists of a signal phrase naming the author (*Civil War historian Dudley Taylor Cornish observes that*) and a page number in parentheses (158).
2. Plagiarized. The student has copied most of the sentence word-for-word from the source without using quotation marks. In addition, the student has failed to document the source with an MLA in-text citation.
3. OK. The student has enclosed borrowed words in quotation marks and has correctly documented the quotation with an MLA in-text citation.
4. Plagiarized. Although the student has used quotation marks around words borrowed from the source, the student has failed to cite the source of the quotations and the page number on which they can be found. The following is an acceptable revision:

   During the Civil War, Dudley Taylor Cornish points out, the Lincoln administration had the "humanity and good sense" not to send "agitators among [the] slaves to incite them to insurrection" (158).
5. OK. The student has paraphrased without using language or structure from the source and has correctly cited the author and page number.

EXERCISE 54-2 Avoiding plagiarism in MLA papers, page 8

1. Plagiarized. The student has copied the sentence word-for-word from the source but has not enclosed it in quotation marks and has not documented it with an MLA in-text citation.
2. OK. The student has put quoted words in quotation marks and has documented the source with an MLA in-text citation consisting of a signal phrase naming the author and a page number in parentheses.
3. Plagiarized. Although the student has correctly documented the source with an MLA in-text citation, the second sentence paraphrases the original source far too closely.
4. OK. This passage is written in the student's own words and is correctly documented with an MLA in-text citation that consists of a signal phrase naming the author and page numbers in parentheses.
5. Plagiarized. Although the student has correctly used an MLA in-text citation, the student has failed to put quoted words in quotation marks.

EXERCISE 54-3 Avoiding plagiarism in MLA papers, page 9

1. Plagiarized. Although the source is cited, the student has paraphrased the source too closely. Simply changing a word or two and switching the order of phrases is not acceptable. A paraphrase must be in the writer's own words.
2. Plagiarized. The student has paraphrased the source too closely by borrowing the sentence structure of the original and then plugging in synonyms (*disseminate* for *spreads out*, *pervade* for *permeate*).
3. OK. In addition to providing a citation, the student has paraphrased the source without borrowing too much language.
4. OK. In addition to providing a citation, the student has enclosed exact language from the source in quotation marks.
5. Plagiarized. Although the source is cited, the student has paraphrased the source too closely and borrowed language from the source (*far-reaching popularity*, for example) without enclosing it in quotation marks.
6. OK. In addition to providing a citation, the student has paraphrased the source without borrowing too much of its language.
7. Plagiarized. In addition to copying from the source almost word-for-word without using quotation marks, the student has failed to cite the author and page number for the source.
8. OK. In addition to providing a signal phrase naming the author and a page number in parentheses, the student has enclosed the source's exact language in quotation marks.
9. Plagiarized. The student has paraphrased the source too closely, has not enclosed borrowed language in quotation marks, and has not given the author and page number.
10. OK. In addition to providing a citation, the student has enclosed exact language from the source in quotation marks.

EXERCISE 54-4 Avoiding plagiarism in MLA papers, page 11

1. Plagiarized. The student uses language borrowed from the original source without quotation marks and without crediting the author. The following is an acceptable revision:
   Rushdie points out that "the sheer number of occasions on which people cry" in *The Wizard of Oz* is astounding (223).
2. OK. The student has paraphrased without using language or structure from the source. The student also cites the

author's name and gives the page numbers for the source in parentheses.
3. Plagiarized. The student has borrowed words from the source without putting them in quotation marks (*tears of frustration, sodden with tears, rusts up again*) and has plugged in synonyms for other language from the source (*cries* for *bawls, hits* for *bops*).
4. OK. The student has correctly placed borrowed language in quotation marks and given the author's name and the page numbers on which the quotation can be found.
5. Plagiarized. The student has used the words *extreme performance* from the source without putting them in quotation marks.

EXERCISE 54-5 Avoiding plagiarism in MLA papers, page 12

1. OK. The student has enclosed the exact words from the source in quotation marks and identifies the author in a signal phrase and the page number in parentheses.
2. OK. The student has paraphrased the source without using its language or structure and has credited the author and cited the page number on which the ideas can be found.
3. Plagiarized. Although the student has credited the source with a signal phrase and a page number in parentheses, the student paraphrases the source too closely, using the same or similar words (*seldom, faithfully, stick, wander*) and borrowing the sentence structure from the source.
4. Plagiarized. The student's paraphrase uses language from the source without quotation marks (*irrelevancies, embarrassed, relevancy*) and a sentence structure that is too close to that in the source. In addition, the student does not credit the author of the ideas or the page number on which they can be found.
5. Plagiarized. The student has used language from the source (*modern ears, wandered all around and arrived nowhere*) without enclosing it in quotation marks.

EXERCISE 54-6 Recognizing common knowledge in MLA papers, page 13

1. Common knowledge. Yoknapatawpha County is mentioned in virtually all sources discussing Faulkner, so his invention of this place can be considered common knowledge.
2. Needs citation. The scholar whose research led to this hypothesis should be given credit.
3. Common knowledge. Information about birth and death dates and the life circumstances of well-known authors usually does not require citation.
4. Needs citation. A reader would not encounter this information repeatedly in books and articles on Shakespeare, so it requires a citation.
5. Needs citation. This information might be considered controversial, especially among admirers of Disney.
6. Common knowledge. This is information that would appear in many sources on Wordsworth and Shelley, so a paper on these poets would not need to cite it.
7. Needs citation. Statistics generally require a citation.
8. Common knowledge. This is a definition of a standard literary form—a type of information found in almost any introductory literature text.
9. Common knowledge. This information about Iris Murdoch is widely known, and a student would find mention of it in most recent sources related to Murdoch.
10. Needs citation. This information would probably be surprising to many readers (and some might doubt its veracity), so a citation is needed.

EXERCISE 55-1 Integrating sources in MLA papers, page 14

1. This sentence is unacceptable. The second part of the sentence is a direct quotation from the source, so it must appear in quotation marks:

    > Wind power accounts for more than 1% of California's electricity, reports Frederic Golden, and "[d]uring breezy early mornings in summer, the contribution goes even higher" (B1).

2. OK. Quoted words appear in quotation marks, and the student provides the author's name in the signal phrase and the page number in parentheses.

3. This passage is unacceptable. The words appearing in quotation marks are not word-for-word accurate. Also, the statement is not accurate because the 8% figure applies only on certain days. The following is an acceptable revision:

    > Mary A. Ilyin reports that under certain weather conditions, "the wind accounts for up to 8%" of California's electricity (qtd. in Golden B1).

4. OK. The brackets indicate that the word *California's* does not appear in the original source, and otherwise the quotation is word-for-word accurate. In addition, the MLA citation correctly indicates that the words belong to Ilyin, who was quoted by Golden.

5. This passage is unacceptable. The second sentence is a dropped quotation. Quotations must be introduced with a signal phrase, usually naming the author. The following is an acceptable revision:

    > California has pioneered the use of wind power. According to Frederic Golden, "Half of California's turbines . . . are located in Altamont Pass" (B1).

EXERCISE 55-2 Integrating sources in MLA papers, page 15

1. The sentence is unacceptable. The student has failed to enclose borrowed language in quotation marks and to introduce the quoted words with a signal phrase naming the authors. The following is an acceptable revision:

    > Burrows and Wallace note that the Delmonico brothers' French restaurant was among the first eating establishments "to let diners order from a menu of choices, at any time they pleased, and sit at their own cloth-covered tables" (437).

2. OK. Quoted words appear in quotation marks, and the student has provided a context for the quotation and named the authors in a signal phrase.

3. OK. The student has enclosed exact words from the source in quotation marks and has introduced the quotation with a signal phrase naming the authors.

4. This passage is unacceptable. The second sentence is a dropped quotation. The student has failed to provide a signal phrase naming the authors. The following is an acceptable revision:

    > In 1830, the Delmonico brothers opened one of the first restaurants in New York City. "This was a sharp break," according to Burrows and Wallace, "from the fixed fare and simultaneous seatings at common hotel tables—so crowded (one guidebook warned) that your elbows were 'pinned down to your sides like the wings of a trussed fowl'" (437).

5. This sentence is unacceptable. The words enclosed in quotation marks are not word-for-word accurate. The following is an acceptable revision:

    > According to Burrows and Wallace, the Delmonico brothers' original shop enticed New Yorkers "with a half-dozen pine tables where customers could sample fine French pastries, coffee, chocolate, wine, and liquor" (437).

6. OK. The student has enclosed words from the source in quotation marks, and the word *such* (added to make the student's sentence grammatical) appears in brackets to indicate that it does not occur in the original source.

7. This passage is unacceptable. The student has borrowed words from the source without enclosing them in quotation marks. The following is an acceptable revision:

    > Burrows and Wallace observe that the Delmonico brothers' restaurant first attracted "resident European agents of export houses, who felt themselves marooned among a people with barbarous eating habits" (437).

8. This sentence is unacceptable. Although the student has enclosed exact language from the source in quotation marks, the student has failed to introduce the quotation with a signal phrase naming the authors. The following is an acceptable revision:

    > Burrows and Wallace observe that the Delmonico brothers' restaurant first attracted "resident European agents of export houses, who felt themselves marooned among a people with barbarous eating habits" (437).

9. OK. The student has enclosed words from the source in quotation marks and indicated changes in the original with brackets and an ellipsis mark.

10. This is a dropped quotation. The student has failed to provide a signal phrase naming the authors. The following is an acceptable revision:

    > Native New Yorkers were at first suspicious of the concept of a restaurant. But as Burrows and Wallace note, "The idea soon caught on, . . . more restaurants appeared, and harried businessmen abandoned the ancient practice of going home for lunch" (437).

EXERCISE 55-3 Integrating sources in MLA papers, page 17

1. OK. The student has put quotation marks around the exact words from the source and has handled the MLA citation correctly, putting the name of the author in a signal phrase and the page number in parentheses.

2. The sentence is unacceptable. The phrase *active safety* is enclosed in quotation marks in the source; single quotation marks are required for a quotation within a quotation. In addition, the student has failed to use an ellipsis mark to indicate that the word *which* is omitted from the quotation. The following is an acceptable revision:

    > Gladwell argues that "'active safety' . . . is every bit as important" as a vehicle's ability to withstand a collision (31).

3. This passage is unacceptable. The second sentence is a dropped quotation. Quotations should be introduced with a signal phrase, usually naming the author. The following is an acceptable revision:

    > A majority of drivers can, indeed, be wrong. As Malcolm Gladwell points out, "Most of us think that S.U.V.s are much safer than sports cars" (31).

4. OK. The student has introduced the quotation with a signal phrase and used brackets to indicate the change from *you* to *they* to fit the grammar of the sentence.

5. This sentence is unacceptable. The student has changed the wording of the source (*of surviving*) to fit the grammar of the sentence (*to survive*) but has not indicated the change with brackets. The following is an acceptable revision:

    > Gladwell explains that most people expect an SUV "[to survive] a collision with a hypothetical tractor-trailer in the other lane" (31).

EXERCISE 55-4 Integrating sources in MLA papers, page 18

1. This sentence is unacceptable. The student has failed to cite the page number on which the quotation appears. The page number should be placed in parentheses after the quotation and before the final period:

    > Packer notes "the liberalization in Africa of the rules governing used-clothing imports in the past ten years" (232).

2. OK. The student has enclosed the exact words of the source in quotation marks and has correctly cited the author in a signal phrase and the page number in parentheses.

3. OK. The student has enclosed direct words from the source in quotation marks and has used "qtd. in" to indicate that the quoted words belong to a person interviewed by the author, not to the author (see item 23 in 56a).

4. This sentence is unacceptable. The student has attributed the ideas in this paraphrase to the author of the passage, but the ideas were expressed by a person the author interviewed, not by the author. The following is an acceptable revision:

    > A Ugandan driver asserts that his culture will not survive for another decade because Ugandans are becoming accustomed to Western goods (Packer 233).

5. This sentence is unacceptable. Although the student has used quotation marks around the quoted passage and has cited the author and page number correctly, the quotation is not word-for-word accurate from the source. In addition, the writer has failed to use brackets to indicate a word changed from the source to fit the grammar of the sentence. The following is an acceptable revision:

    > An American reporter observes that the availability of Western clothing may send Africans the message that "their own things are worthless, that [they] can do nothing for themselves" (Packer 233).

EXERCISE 56-1 MLA documentation: in-text citations, page 19

1. a. In MLA style, the sentence period comes after the parenthetical citation.

2. b. When a work has two or three authors, all authors must be named either in a signal phrase or in the parenthetical citation.

3. b. When the author of an article is unknown, a short form of the title is given in the parenthetical citation.

4. a. A short form of the title of the work appears in the parenthetical citation because two works by Marshall are given in the works cited list.

5. b. The author's name is not given in the signal phrase (*According to one expert*), so it appears in the parenthetical citation along with a short form of the title of the work and the page number on which the quotation may be found.

6. a. For an unpaginated online source, a signal phrase giving the author of the source is sufficient. The abbreviation "n. pag." is not necessary.

7. a. The signal phrase gives the complete name of the author of the source, in this case a government agency. If the student uses a parenthetical citation, it must include the complete name under which the work is given in the list of works cited: (United States, Dept. of Justice, Drug Enforcement Administration).

8. a. When a source is quoted in another source, MLA style requires the abbreviation "qtd. in" (for "quoted in").

9. b. Because the question mark is in the original source, it appears inside the quotation mark and before the parenthetical citation. A period follows the parentheses.

10. a. In MLA style for a work with more than three authors, the in-text citation matches the entry in the list of works cited. In this case, "et al." appears after the first author's name. Alternatively, the student could use all the authors' names in the works cited list and the in-text citation.

EXERCISE 56-2 MLA documentation: in-text citations, page 23

1. b. In MLA style, an in-text citation appears after the quoted material and before the sentence period.

2. a. In MLA style for a source with two authors, both authors' names are given in the signal phrase.

3. a. When two or more works are cited in the same parentheses, the authors' names are separated by a semicolon.

4. a. The author of the work being quoted, not the editor of the collection containing the work, is given in an MLA in-text citation.

5. b. When a paper includes two or more works by the same author, the parenthetical citation includes a short form of the source's title along with the page number.

6. b. Orlean is quoting the town historian, so the parenthetical citation includes the abbreviation "qtd. in" to indicate that the words are not Orlean's.

7. a. The in-text citation for a newspaper article includes the exact page number on which the quotation appears.

8. a. For an unpaginated electronic source, a signal phrase naming the author of the work is sufficient in an MLA in-text citation.

9. b. In MLA style, a work with no author is cited with a short form of its title.

10. b. A work with no author is cited by its title in an MLA in-text citation.

EXERCISE 56-3 MLA documentation: in-text citations, page 27

1. a. The author's name is given in the signal phrase, and the page number is given in the parenthetical citation.

2. a. The citation names the author of the work being quoted, not the editor of the book.

3. a. When a long quotation is indented in MLA style, quotation marks are not used to enclose the quotation; the parenthetical citation comes after the end punctuation of the quotation.

4. b. When the works cited list includes two works by the same author, the citation includes a title (or a short form of the title) of the work.

5. a. The signal phrase (*Mayer claims . . .*) names the author of the essay; the editors of the anthology are not given in the in-text citation.

6. b. For unpaginated material from a Web site, a signal phrase naming the author of the work is sufficient in an MLA in-text citation.

7. a. When a work has fewer than four authors, all names are listed in the in-text citation.

8. b. When a source has a known author, the author is included in the signal phrase or in a parenthetical citation. (Page numbers are not given because the work is from an unpaginated online source.)

9. a. Because Twain's words appear in an article written by someone else (a secondary source), the abbreviation "qtd. in" is used in the parenthetical citation before the author of the secondary source.

10. a. Both authors' names are included in the parenthetical citation. (A page number is not required in this citation because the article was accessed in a database that does not show page breaks.)

EXERCISE 56-4 MLA documentation: identifying elements of sources, page 31

1. b. The author of the site is Harry Rusche. The line at the bottom of the main page states that he created the site.
2. b. Harry Rusche is given as the creator of the site, so the entry should begin with his name.
3. b. Only the year is given in parentheses, and the first page number is followed by a plus sign to indicate that the article continues after the first page.
4. a. The works cited entry should include the name of the database, the medium ("Web"), and the date of access.
5. b. In the title of a book in MLA style, only the principal words (nouns, pronouns, adjectives, and verbs) are capitalized, regardless of the capitalization that appears on the title page.
6. b. Only the first city on the title page is given in the works cited entry, and the state is not used.
7. a. The abbreviation "P" (for "Press") is omitted because the publisher is not a university press, and the medium ("Print") is included.
8. a. The author of the poem is listed first and the speaker (narrator) is listed after the title of the work.
9. b. As author of the essay you are citing, Baudrillard would appear first in the works cited entry.
10. b. The date of publication of the essay itself should not be included in the works cited entry. The date of publication of the anthology (not shown) should be included in the entry.

EXERCISE 56-5 MLA documentation: works cited, page 37

1. a. For a work with no author, a works cited entry begins with the title of the source, not with "Anonymous."
2. a. In MLA style, a work with four or more authors is listed by the name of the first author followed by "et al." (Latin for "and others"). Alternatively, a work can be listed by the names of all the authors as they are given in the source.
3. a. In MLA style, an imprint (division) of a publisher precedes the publisher's name in the works cited entry.
4. b. Because the student has used dialogue from the film and has not emphasized one person's contribution, the MLA works cited entry begins with the title of the film, not the director's name.
5. b. The sponsor, the date of publication, and the date of access are given for an online source.
6. a. Although the student has quoted Towne's words, the book in which the words appear was written by Biskind, not Towne.
7. a. The works cited entry for a review should include the words "Rev. of" and the title and author of the work reviewed.
8. b. In MLA style for dates, the day precedes the month, and the day and the month are not separated from the year with a comma.
9. b. In MLA style, the authors' names are followed by the title of the article and then the name of the newspaper, the date, and the page number.
10. a. In MLA style, when the author of a work is unknown, the works cited entry begins with the work's title. The term "Anonymous" is not used.

EXERCISE 56-6 MLA documentation: works cited, page 39

1. a. In an MLA works cited entry, when a work has more than one author, the first author's name is given in reverse order, last name first. The names of other authors are given in normal order.
2. a. In an MLA works cited entry, the names of all months except May, June, and July are abbreviated.

3. b. When a works cited list contains more than one source by the same author, the works are listed alphabetically, with the author's name given in the first entry and three hyphens in place of the author's name in subsequent entries. This is the second entry, so three hyphens appear in place of the author's name.
4. a. Because this encyclopedia is not well known, the works cited entry includes complete publication information. Note that when a work is published jointly, both cities and publishers are included, separated by a semicolon.
5. a. Because the student has quoted from the foreword of the book, the foreword and its author are given first in the MLA works cited entry.
6. b. The sponsor of the site must be named in the works cited entry, even if it is the same as the Web site title.
7. a. An MLA works cited entry for a part of a work, such as a chapter, includes the page numbers on which the part of the work appears.
8. a. In an MLA works cited entry for a work from a Web site, the sponsor of the site is given before the date of publication.
9. b. Because the student has used dialogue from the film and has not emphasized one person's contribution, the MLA works cited entry begins with the title of the film, not the director's name.
10. a. An MLA works cited entry for a review includes the words "Rev. of" along with relevant information about the work being reviewed.

EXERCISE 56-7 MLA documentation: works cited, page 43

1. b. Citations for government documents begin with the name of the government, the department or the branch of government, and the agency or committee.
2. b. When a source is retrieved from a library's subscription database, the name of the database (in this case, *Academic Search Premier*) is included in the citation.
3. a. When citing a single work from an anthology, the individual work is listed first, beginning with its author's name. (The abbreviation "Ed." stands for "Edited by," so it is the same for one or multiple editors.)
4. b. When two or more works are used from the same anthology, an entry for the entire anthology is provided along with shortened entries for each selection. Entries are listed alphabetically by authors' last names.
5. a. In an entry from an encyclopedia or a dictionary, volume and page numbers are not necessary because the entries in the source are arranged alphabetically.
6. a. When citing a program accessed online, the title of the Web site (in this case, *msnbc.com*) is included after the network and the date of posting.
7. b. DVD titles appear in italics.
8. a. Since the publisher of the site is listed as Times-Picayune, that should be included in the entry.
9. b. The blog has no sponsor, so the abbreviation "N.p." (for "No publisher") is used.
10. b. When the author of a short work from a Web site is unknown, the entry begins with the title of the work, and the sponsor of the site is listed after the Web site title.

EXERCISE 56-8 MLA documentation, page 46

1. False. The work's title isn't always necessary. In an in-text citation, the title is needed only if the work has no author or if two or more works by the same author appear in the list of works cited. Page numbers are not necessary for sources from the Web and the other unpaginated sources.

2. True. The alphabetical organization helps readers quickly find the source that has been cited in the text.
3. False. The list should include only the works the writer has cited in the paper.
4. True. MLA provides an option for including the author's name: It can appear in a signal phrase or in parentheses.
5. False. When a work's author is unknown, the work is listed under its title.
6. False. The list is titled Works Cited.
7. True. If the author is named in a signal phrase, it is possible that nothing will appear in parentheses.
8. False. MLA style does not use any abbreviation before the page number.
9. True. Because more than one work will appear in the works cited list, the title is necessary for identifying the exact work that has been cited. The author's name is not enough.
10. True. Because Web sources may change, the date of access is needed.

EXERCISE 58-1 Thesis statements in APA papers, page 47

1. b. This sentence asserts a specific cause and effect that can be developed into an argument. The other sentence is a vague prediction that would be difficult to support with scientific evidence.
2. a. This sentence calls for a clear course of action that can be defended in an argument. The other sentence is vague because it does not call for a course of action and too broad because it includes all consumers.
3. a. This sentence suggests that the paper will examine reasons for police reluctance to adopt a new system. The other sentence is too vague to be an acceptable thesis.
4. b. This sentence offers an assertion that can be developed into an argument. The other sentence simply states a fact.
5. a. This sentence presents an idea that can be argued in a paper. The other sentence simply lists symptoms of a disorder.
6. b. This sentence focuses on a causal connection between images and eating disorders. The other sentence is too broad to develop in depth.
7. b. This sentence offers an assertion that can be argued in a paper. The other sentence simply states a fact.
8. a. This sentence focuses on specific benefits that can be discussed in a paper. The other sentence is too vague.
9. a. This sentence focuses on one program and argues that it has not worked as planned. The other sentence is too broad because it tries to cover very different kinds of programs, and it is too vague because it does not specify what "more harm than good" means.
10. b. This sentence makes a clear and specific assertion about an arguable matter. The other sentence is too broad.

EXERCISE 58-2 Thesis statements in APA papers, page 49

1. b. This statement makes an assertion about homeschooling that can be developed in a paper. The other statement is a statistic; it is too factual to be an effective thesis.
2. a. This statement makes an assertion about the child care industry that can be supported with evidence in a paper. The other statement is too vague to be an effective thesis.
3. b. This statement takes a position on gambling revenues that can be argued in a paper. The other statement is too factual to be an effective thesis.
4. a. This statement makes an assertion about the validity of one particular theory, and this assertion can be argued in a paper. The other statement is too factual to be an effective thesis.

5. a. This statement makes a focused assertion about antidepressants that can be supported with evidence in a paper. The other statement is too broad and vague to be an effective thesis.
6. b. This statement makes a claim based on "recent evidence," setting up a paper that can discuss this evidence and argue a position. The other sentence merely states a fact about what parents want and would not make an effective thesis.
7. b. This statement is a call to action; it makes an assertion about suicide rates that can be argued in a paper. The other statement makes a claim that is too vague to be an effective thesis.
8. a. This statement makes a focused claim about standardized tests that can be supported with evidence in a paper. The other statement would not make an effective thesis because it lacks focus and assertiveness; it broadly summarizes two opposing viewpoints on NCLB without taking a stand on either one.
9. b. This statement makes an assertion about teacher salaries that can be supported with evidence in a paper. The other statement is too factual to be an effective thesis.
10. a. This statement is a call to action; it makes an assertion about the need for mental health care in military families that can be argued in a paper. The other statement makes a claim that is too factual to be an effective thesis.

EXERCISE 59-1 Avoiding plagiarism in APA papers, page 51

1. Plagiarized. The student uses the source's exact words without enclosing them in quotation marks.
2. OK. The student has correctly enclosed a direct quotation from the source in quotation marks and has cited the source properly.
3. Plagiarized. The student has paraphrased the original too closely, borrowing both phrases and structure from the original.
4. OK. The student has paraphrased the source without using language or structure from the source and has correctly cited the paraphrase.
5. OK. The student has correctly enclosed the exact words of the source in quotation marks and has correctly cited the author's name, the date, and the page number.
6. Plagiarized. Although the student has cited the source correctly, the student has paraphrased too closely, borrowing both phrases and structure from the original.
7. OK. The student has paraphrased the source without using borrowed structure or phrases and has cited the source correctly.
8. OK. The student has paraphrased the source without borrowing language or structure and has correctly cited the source.
9. Plagiarized. Although the student has cited the source correctly, the student has used the source almost word-for-word without quotation marks.
10. Plagiarized. The student has paraphrased the source too closely, using the structure of the original and plugging in occasional synonyms (*dupe* for *fool*, *co-workers* for *others*, *supposedly* for *presumably*).

EXERCISE 59-2 Avoiding plagiarism in APA papers, page 53

1. Plagiarized. The student has copied chunks of text from the source word-for-word without enclosing the borrowed words in quotation marks and without providing a citation.
2. Plagiarized. Although the student has cited the source, the paraphrase is too close to the structure and language of the original.

3. OK. In addition to citing the source, the student has enclosed exact words from the source in quotation marks.
4. OK. In addition to citing the source, the student has enclosed exact words from the source in quotation marks.
5. OK. In addition to citing the source, the student has paraphrased it without borrowing too much of its language.
6. Plagiarized. Although a borrowed phrase correctly appears in quotation marks, the student has paraphrased the source too closely, borrowing structure from the original and plugging in synonyms (*ill* for *sick*, *not at all what you would expect in* for *quite different from*, *ailment* for *illness*).
7. Plagiarized. Although the sentence begins as an acceptable paraphrase, it ends by using the source almost word-for-word without quotation marks.
8. OK. In addition to citing the source, the student has paraphrased it without borrowing too much of its language.
9. Plagiarized. In addition to copying the source almost word-for-word without using quotation marks, the student has failed to cite the author, year, and page number for the source.
10. OK. In addition to citing the source, the student has paraphrased it without borrowing too much of its language.

EXERCISE 59-3 Avoiding plagiarism in APA papers, page 55

1. Plagiarized. The student uses words from the source without putting them in quotation marks and does not cite the source.
2. Plagiarized. Although the student has cited the author, date, and page number for the source, the student has paraphrased the source too closely, using sentence structure from the source, plugging in synonyms (*plausible model* for *plausibility of this model*), and rearranging rather than paraphrasing language from the source (*deforestation, industrial pollution, hunting* instead of *hunting, deforestation, and industrial pollution*).
3. OK. The student has paraphrased the source without using the structure or language of the source. In addition, the student has put exact words from the source in quotation marks and has cited the source properly.
4. OK. The student has placed borrowed language in quotation marks and has cited the source of the quotation according to APA style.
5. OK. The writer has put exact language from the source in quotation marks, has paraphrased the rest of the sentence appropriately, and has cited the author, date, and page number in parentheses.

EXERCISE 59-4 Avoiding plagiarism in APA papers, page 56

1. Plagiarized. Although the student has correctly cited the source, the student has failed to enclose in quotation marks all the words taken from the source. The following is an acceptable revision:
   Diamond (2004) explained that the 11 territories on Easter Island were "loosely integrated religiously, economically, and politically under the leadership of one paramount chief" (p. 8).
2. OK. The student has paraphrased the source without using language or structure from the source. The student also has used a parenthetical citation in proper APA style.
3. OK. The student has enclosed exact words from the source in quotation marks and has cited the quotation properly in APA style.
4. Plagiarized. The student has borrowed the sentence structure of the source and has substituted synonyms for many words (*status* for *prestige*, *island-to-island endeavors* for *inter-island efforts*, for instance).

5. Plagiarized. The student has used exact words from the source without enclosing them in quotation marks and has failed to cite the page number from which the words were borrowed. The following is an acceptable revision:
   Diamond (2004) noted that rather than competing with chiefs on other Polynesian islands, Easter Island's chiefs competed among themselves "by erecting statues representing their high-ranking ancestors" (p. 8).

EXERCISE 59-5 Recognizing common knowledge in APA papers, page 57

1. Needs citation. The results of a scientific study such as the trial of a drug should be cited.
2. Common knowledge. This fact was reported in media sources in 2012 with great regularity; it can be considered common knowledge.
3. Needs citation. Although readers may have anecdotal evidence of the popularity of particular baby names, certain knowledge of the number-one name generally requires investigation. The source should be cited.
4. Needs citation. This information is probably known only to specialists. The source should be cited.
5. Common knowledge. An awareness of the connection between taste and smell is common, if only because many people have noticed how a temporary loss of the sense of smell affects their ability to taste.
6. Needs citation. While the existence of the Homestead Act might be considered common knowledge, the statistical fact that women filed 10% of the claims must be cited.
7. Common knowledge. This fact is widely known even outside of the field of baseball (or sports). Information about major records in sports is found in many different sources.
8. Common knowledge. This information is mentioned in most discussions of earthquakes and California. It is a well-known fact that does not require citation.
9. Needs citation. Information that presents the findings of a study—particularly findings that go against the prevailing wisdom—should be cited.
10. Common knowledge. This information can be found in any number of sources, so it does not need a citation.

EXERCISE 60-1 Integrating sources in APA papers, page 59

1. This sentence is unacceptable. Although the student has cited the author, date, and page number for the source, the student has used the exact words of the source without quotation marks. The following is an acceptable revision:
   Researchers at Utrecht University found that bereaved spouses "who often talked with others and briefly wrote in diaries about their emotions fared no better than their tight-lipped, unexpressive counterparts" (Bower, 2002, p. 131).
2. This sentence is unacceptable. Although the student has used quotation marks and has cited the source correctly, the student has omitted words from the source (*about their emotions*) without using the ellipsis mark. The following is an acceptable revision:
   Researchers at Utrecht University found that bereaved spouses "who often talked with others and briefly wrote in diaries . . . fared no better than their tight-lipped, unexpressive counterparts" (Bower, 2002, p. 131).
3. OK. The student has put the source's exact words in quotation marks and has used the ellipsis mark to indicate that some words from the source have been omitted.
4. This sentence is unacceptable. The quotation is not word-for-word accurate from the source: The student has changed *have long theorized* to *have always believed* and *the*

death of a loved one to *a loved one's death*. The following is an acceptable revision:

> According to Bower (2002), "Mental-health workers have long theorized that it takes grueling emotional exertion to recover from the death of a loved one" (p. 131).

5. This passage is unacceptable. The student has dropped the quotation into the text without using a signal phrase naming the author. The following is an acceptable revision:

> Mental health professionals have assumed that people stricken by grief need a great deal of help. Bower (2002) pointed out that "so-called grief work, now the stock-in-trade of a growing number of grief counselors, entails confronting the reality of a loved one's demise and grappling with the harsh emotions triggered by that loss" (p. 131).

Note that it is acceptable to change the capital *S* to lower-case at the beginning of the quotation to fit the grammar of the student's sentence.

6. OK. The student has introduced the quotation with a signal phrase naming the author and giving the date in parentheses and has placed the exact words from the source in quotation marks.

7. OK. The student has enclosed language from the source in quotation marks and has used brackets to indicate that words from the source have been changed to fit the grammar of the student's sentence (*confronting* changed to *confront*, *grappling* changed to *grapple*).

8. This sentence is unacceptable. In APA style, the verb in a signal phrase should be in the past or the past perfect tense (*found* or *have found*), not the present tense (*find*). The following is an acceptable revision:

> Researchers at Utrecht University have found no difference in the speed of adapting to a spouse's death among subjects "who often talked with others and briefly wrote in diaries" and "their tight-lipped, unexpressive counterparts" (Bower, 2002, p. 131).

9. This passage is unacceptable. Although the student has used a correct APA-style signal phrase and has put the page number in parentheses following the quotation, the student should not have used quotation marks to enclose a long quotation that is set off from the text by indenting. The following is an acceptable revision:

> Bower (2002) noted that new studies may change the common perception of how people recover from grief:
>
> > Among bereaved spouses tracked for up to 2 years after their partners' death, those who often talked with others and briefly wrote in diaries about their emotions fared no better than their tight-lipped, unexpressive counterparts, according to psychologist Margaret Stroebe of Utrecht University in the Netherlands and her colleagues. (p. 131)

10. OK. The student has enclosed borrowed language in quotation marks and has used an ellipsis mark to indicate that the word *however* has been omitted from the source. The student also has used a proper APA signal phrase and parenthetical citation.

EXERCISE 60-2 Integrating sources in APA papers, page 61

1. OK. The student has introduced the quotation with a signal phrase naming the author and giving the date in parentheses and has enclosed borrowed language in quotation marks.

2. This sentence is unacceptable. The student has changed words in the quotation (*of them* to *convicted sex offenders*) without enclosing the changed words in brackets. The following is an acceptable revision:

> Bower (2002) reported a surprising finding based on several longitudinal studies: "Many [convicted sex offenders] don't return to their criminal ways" (p. 60).

3. This passage is unacceptable. Although the student has used an APA-style parenthetical citation, the student has dropped the quotation into the text without a signal phrase. The following is an acceptable revision:

> No one has yet answered the question of how to deal with potentially dangerous sex offenders who are serving prison time. As Bower (2002) has pointed out, "Researchers are attempting to come up with statistical tools that courts can use to decide who should stay behind bars and who should go free" (p. 60).

4. OK. The student has prepared readers for the quotation by naming the author and providing some context for the author's words.

5. This sentence is unacceptable. The student has failed to use quotation marks around a passage borrowed word-for-word from the source. The following is an acceptable revision:

> A Canadian psychologist has reported that "data from several long-term studies of 4,724 sex offenders released from prisons in the United States and Canada after 1980 show that after 10 years, one in five had been arrested for a new sexual offense" (Bower, 2002, p. 60).

Note that it is acceptable to change the capital *D* to lower-case at the beginning of the quotation to fit the grammar of the student's sentence.

6. OK. The student has put exact words from the source in quotation marks and has used an ellipsis mark to indicate that some words from the source have been omitted.

7. This sentence is unacceptable. The student has changed part of the sentence in quotation marks without indicating the changes with an ellipsis mark or brackets. The following is an acceptable revision:

> As long-term studies have indicated, "Among men who had victimized children in their own families, . . . [only about 10%] committed a new sexual offense during the first 20 years after release from prison" (Bower, 2002, p. 60).

8. OK. The student has enclosed borrowed language in quotation marks and has used brackets to indicate that a word from the source has been changed (*victimized* to *victimizing*). The student also has used an ellipsis mark to show that a phrase was omitted from the source.

9. This passage is unacceptable. Although the student has used a correct APA-style signal phrase and has put the page number in parentheses following the quotation, the student should not have used quotation marks to enclose a long quotation that is set off from the text by indenting. The following is an acceptable revision:

> Bower (2002) provided evidence that sex offenders do not always repeat their crimes after serving sentences:
>
> > Data from several long-term studies of 4,724 sex offenders released from prisons in the United States and Canada after 1980 show that after 10 years, one in five had been arrested for a new sexual offense, says psychologist R. Karl Hanson of the Department of the Solicitor General of Canada in Ottawa. After 20 years, that figure rose to slightly more than one in four. (p. 60)

10. OK. The student has introduced the quotation with a signal phrase and has placed exact words from the source in quotation marks. The words *as cited in Bower* indicate that Hanson is quoted in the article by Bower.

EXERCISE 60-3 Integrating sources in APA papers, page 63

1. This sentence is unacceptable. In APA style, the date should appear in parentheses immediately after the author's name:

   According to Kidder (1989), "teachers learn through experience, but they learn without much guidance" (p. 51).

2. This sentence is unacceptable. The student has omitted words (*both, can*) and changed words (*hardens* for *harden*) from the original source without indicating the changes with the ellipsis mark or brackets. The following is an acceptable revision:

   Kidder (1989) argued that teaching experience, "especially the kind that is . . . repetitive and disappointing, . . . easily harden[s] into narrow pedagogical theories" (p. 51).

3. OK. The student has placed borrowed language in quotation marks and has correctly cited the date and page number for the source.

4. This sentence is unacceptable. The student has failed to integrate the quotation in a grammatical sentence. The following is an acceptable revision:

   In the view of Kidder (1989), it's not unusual for a teacher to have "a theory built on grudges" (p. 51).

5. This sentence is unacceptable. The student has dropped the quotation into the text without using a signal phrase naming the author. The following is an acceptable revision:

   Kidder (1989) asserted that most teachers gain experience on the job and develop rigid habits and theories after as few as four years. But, he continued, "many teachers don't last that long" (p. 51).

EXERCISE 60-4 Integrating sources in APA papers, page 64

1. OK. The student has placed borrowed language in quotation marks and has integrated the borrowed material smoothly into the sentence.

2. OK. The student has placed borrowed language in quotation marks and has used an ellipsis mark to indicate that the word *remember* is omitted.

3. This passage is unacceptable. The second sentence is a dropped quotation: The writer has failed to introduce it with a signal phrase naming the author. The following is an acceptable revision:

   Many people believe that the home environment has a direct effect on the way children grow up. Pinker (2003) asserted, however, that "the conclusions depend on the belief that children are blank slates" (p. 39).

4. This passage is unacceptable. The student has failed to use an ellipsis mark to indicate that the words *to grow the best children* were omitted from the source. The following is an acceptable revision:

   As Pinker (2003) has pointed out, "Everyone concludes that . . . parents must be loving, authoritative, and talkative, and if children don't turn out well it must be the parents' fault. But the conclusions depend on the belief that children are blank slates" (p. 39).

5. This sentence is unacceptable. The student has used the quotation in a misleading way. Pinker in fact disputes this belief. The following is an acceptable revision:

   Pinker (2003) countered "the belief that children are blank slates" by asserting that genes play as much a role as environment in raising children.

EXERCISE 61-1 APA documentation: in-text citations, page 65

1. b. In APA style, the period comes after the parenthetical citation.

2. a. In an APA parenthetical citation for a work with two authors, an ampersand (&) is placed between the authors' names.

3. b. In APA style, when the author's name is given in a signal phrase, the name is followed by the date in parentheses.

4. b. In APA style for a work with three to five authors, the signal phrase includes all the authors' last names the first time the source is cited. For subsequent citations of the source, "et al." is used after the first author's name.

5. a. In APA style, the word "and" joins two authors' names in a signal phrase; the ampersand (&) is used in a parenthetical citation.

6. a. In APA style, two or more works by the same author in the same year are listed alphabetically by the first word of the title (other than *A, An,* or *The*) in the list of references. A lowercase letter is added to the year, with "a" for the first and "b" for the second reference by the author in that year. The lowercase letter is also used with the year in the in-text citation.

7. a. In APA style, when an electronic source has numbered paragraphs but not page numbers, the parenthetical citation includes the abbreviation "para." and the paragraph number.

8. b. For a source without a date, the abbreviation "n.d." is used in the parenthetical citation.

9. a. The National Science Board is listed as the author in the reference list, so it appears with the date in the signal phrase. "Anonymous" is not used in this case.

10. a. When information is taken from more than one consecutive page in the source, the range of pages is given.

EXERCISE 61-2 APA documentation: in-text citations, page 69

1. b. In APA style, the abbreviation "p." appears before the page number in parentheses.

2. a. In an APA parenthetical citation for a work with two authors, an ampersand (&) is placed between the authors' names.

3. a. In APA style, the word "and" joins two authors' names in a signal phrase; the ampersand (&) is used in a parenthetical citation.

4. a. The abbreviation "p." and the page number should be given in parentheses after a quotation whenever a page number is available.

5. b. Two or more works by the same author in the same year are listed alphabetically by title in the reference list. A lowercase letter ("a," "b," and so on) is added after the year to indicate the order in the list, and the letter is also used after the year in the in-text citation.

6. a. Because the Web site is divided into named sections, the student has cited the title of the section along with the number of the paragraph within the section.

7. a. In an APA in-text citation, the period comes after the parentheses.

8. b. In APA style, when the author's name is given in a signal phrase, the name is followed by the date in parentheses.

9. a. In APA style for a work with three to five authors, the signal phrase includes all the authors' last names the first time the source is cited. For subsequent citations of the source, "et al." is used after the first author's name.

10. a. For a source without a date, the abbreviation "n.d." is used in a parenthetical citation.

EXERCISE 61-3 APA documentation: in-text citations, page 73

1. b. The year alone, without the month and day, is used in an APA in-text citation of a newspaper article.

2. a. When a source has two authors, the names are joined with an ampersand (&) in the parenthetical citation.
3. b. An APA in-text citation gives the exact page number where the quotation is found.
4. b. When a paper includes more than one work by the same author in the same year, the in-text citation gives the year followed by the letter. The title of the work is not included.
5. a. For a work with three to five authors, the first citation of the source lists all the authors' names, and subsequent citations use the first author's name followed by "et al."

EXERCISE 61-4 APA documentation: identifying elements of sources, page 75

1. a. The author's first and middle names are given by initials only, and the date of publication given is the most recent date on the copyright page.
2. b. In APA style, only the first word of the title, the first word after a colon, and proper nouns are capitalized, and the edition number follows the book title.
3. a. The name of the author of the chapter appears first in the reference list entry.
4. b. The author and title of the individual work appear first in the reference list entry. In addition, the book and chapter titles are capitalized correctly in APA style.
5. a. The author's name is given first, and the title of the article is not enclosed in quotation marks.
6. a. Both the volume number and the issue number are given because each issue begins on page 1. (The year follows the author's name, not the volume number.)
7. b. If a database record contains a DOI (digital object identifier), the DOI is sufficient at the end of a reference list entry.
8. b. In APA style, the title of a blog post is not italicized. And the label "Blog post" is included in brackets following the title of the post.
9. b. The term "Insights" is a title for the section of the magazine and is not part of the article title.
10. a. In an APA reference list entry for a monthly magazine, the month, the year, and the volume number are included. The issue number is included when each issue of the magazine begins on page 1, as in this case.

EXERCISE 61-5 APA documentation: reference list, page 81

1. b. In a book title in an APA reference list, only the first word of the title and the first word of the subtitle (and any proper nouns) are capitalized.
2. b. For a work with two authors in an APA reference list, both authors' names are given last name first, followed by initial(s).
3. a. When a source has seven authors or fewer, all of the authors' names are given in an APA reference list. The abbreviation "et al." is not used.
4. a. For a newspaper article that does not appear on consecutive pages, the APA reference list entry includes all page numbers on which parts of the article are found.
5. a. When a paper cites more than one work by an author in the same year, the works are arranged alphabetically by title in the APA reference list. The year in parentheses is followed by lowercase letters beginning with "a," "b," and so on, corresponding to the works' order in the list.
6. a. In an APA reference list, the issue number is not included if the journal or magazine is paginated by volume.
7. b. In APA style, the URL for an online magazine article should be for the home page of the magazine.
8. a. If an article accessed through a database does not have a DOI (digital object identifier), then the URL for the home

page of the magazine (not the database number) should be given in the reference list entry.
9. a. An APA reference list entry for a review of a book contains the words "Review of the book," followed by the title of the book and the author's name in brackets.
10. b. Personal communications are cited in the text of an APA paper, but they are not included in the reference list.

EXERCISE 61-6 APA documentation: reference list, page 85

1. a. The reference list entry for a work with no author begins with the title of the work.
2. b. In APA reference entries, the identification of the main contributors is put in parentheses.
3. a. The abbreviation "p." is used before the page number of a newspaper article.
4. a. An APA reference entry for a journal article includes the page range of the article, not only the page cited in the paper.
5. a. The abbreviation "Eds." (for "Editors") is included after the editors' names in APA reference entries.
6. b. When a DOI is available for an article accessed in a database, the DOI (not the database name) is included in an APA reference list entry.
7. a. APA reference list entries for articles in scholarly journals list only the year (not the season, month, or day) in parentheses.
8. b. For an audio file with a publication date, a retrieval date is not included in the APA reference list entry.
9. b. The word "Abstract" is included in brackets after the article title.
10. a. For a dissertation accessed from a database, the description "Doctoral dissertation" appears in parentheses following the title and the accession number is included at the end of the entry.

EXERCISE 61-7 APA documentation: reference list, page 89

1. a. When a government agency or another organization serves as both the author and the publisher, the publisher is given as "Author" in the APA reference list entry.
2. b. When an advertisement is cited in an APA reference entry, the word "Advertisement" (not the type of product) appears in brackets after the product name.
3. a. An APA reference list entry for an article in an online newspaper ends with the URL for the home page of the newspaper.
4. b. When a source has eight or more authors, the first six authors are listed, followed by three ellipsis dots and the last author's name.
5. b. In APA reference lists, page numbers are not included for citations to books.
6. a. When no DOI is available for a journal article accessed in a database, the URL for the journal's home page is included in the APA reference list entry.
7. a. APA reference list entries for articles in scholarly journals list only the year (not the season, month, or day) in parentheses.
8. a. The label "Audio podcast" follows the title of the podcast in brackets.
9. b. In an APA reference list entry for an online video file that is not dated, the abbreviation "n.d." (for "no date") is placed in parentheses.
10. b. In an APA reference list entry for a published interview, the person being interviewed is listed first, and the interviewer is named in brackets after the title of the article.

EXERCISE 61-8 APA documentation, page 92

1. False. Although a page number is required for all quotations, it is not necessary for paraphrases and summaries except when providing one would help readers find the passage in a long work.
2. True. Because of these requirements, APA documentation style is sometimes called the "author/date" system.
3. True. The alphabetical organization helps readers quickly find the source that has been cited in the text.
4. False. An ampersand is used only in the parentheses following the citation; in a signal phrase, the word "and" is used.
5. True. Although some other documentation styles omit these abbreviations, APA requires them.
6. False. APA recommends using the past or the past perfect tense (for example, "Baker reported that" or "Wu has argued that").
7. True. The works are listed alphabetically by title, with the first work assigned "a," the second "b," and so on. In-text citations and the list of references both use this designation.
8. True. Because APA is a scientific style, dates are important; even if no date is available, the fact must be noted.
9. False. In an APA reference list, "et al." is never used. If a work has eight or more authors, the names of the first six authors are given, followed by three ellipsis dots and the last author's name.
10. True. The title is used in place of the author's name unless "Anonymous" is actually given as the author in the source.

EXERCISE 63-1 Thesis statements in *Chicago* papers, page 93

1. a. This sentence can be developed into an argument about the importance of the discovery of anesthesia. The other sentence simply states a fact.
2. b. This sentence focuses on one famous explorer and makes an assertion that can be argued in a paper. The other sentence is too broad.
3. b. This sentence makes an assertion that can be developed into an argument about the value of film preservation. The other sentence simply states a fact.
4. a. This sentence makes a clear, focused point that can be argued in a paper. The other sentence is too vague to assert an arguable point.
5. a. This statement can be developed into an argument that explains why a government action in World War II was misguided. The other sentence simply states a fact.
6. a. This sentence makes an assertion for which evidence can be presented. The other sentence is too broad to be a useful thesis statement.
7. b. This sentence asserts an idea that can be argued in a paper. The other sentence is too factual.
8. b. This sentence presents an assertion for which evidence can be presented in a paper.
9. a. This sentence makes an assertion that can be argued in the paper. The other sentence merely states historical facts.
10. b. This sentence is focused, and it makes an arguable assertion. The other sentence is too broad because it covers many decades and hundreds of cities and towns.

EXERCISE 63-2 Thesis statements in *Chicago* papers, page 95

1. b. This statement sets up a cause-and-effect claim that can be supported with evidence in a paper. The other statement is too vague and speculative to be an effective thesis.
2. b. This statement presents an argument that can be developed and supported in a paper. The other statement merely defines what the Elgin marbles are; it is too factual to make an effective thesis.

3. a. This statement makes a claim that focuses on one particular president and the historical context of his scandal. The other statement is vague and too broad to make an effective thesis for a five-to-ten-page paper.
4. b. This statement makes an assertion about what made the American perspective change. The other statement is too factual to be an effective thesis.
5. a. This statement makes an assertion about the missionaries and sets up an argument that can be supported with evidence in a paper. The other statement is too broad to be an effective thesis.
6. b. This statement makes a claim about the nuns that can be supported with evidence in a paper. The other statement is too factual to be an effective thesis.
7. b. This statement makes an assertion about the success of the Chinese Communist Party that can be supported with evidence in a paper. The other statement is too factual to be an effective thesis.
8. a. This statement makes an assertion about US preparedness that can be supported with evidence in a paper. The other statement is too vague to be an effective thesis.
9. b. This statement makes an assertion about the British withdrawal that can be supported with evidence in a paper. The other statement is too vague to be an effective thesis.
10. b. This statement makes an assertion about the protests that can be supported with evidence in a paper. The other statement is too factual to be an effective thesis.

EXERCISE 63-3 Avoiding plagiarism in *Chicago* papers, page 97

1. Plagiarized. Although the student has correctly documented the source with a footnote, the student has paraphrased the source too closely.
2. OK. The student has used quotation marks to indicate exact words from the source and has included a footnote.
3. OK. The student has paraphrased without using language or structure from the source and has cited the source with a footnote.
4. Plagiarized. The student has quoted part of the sentence word-for-word without using quotation marks.
5. Plagiarized. The student has quoted the source word-for-word without using quotation marks and has failed to name the author and provide a footnote.
6. OK. The student has paraphrased without using language or structure from the source and has cited the source with a footnote.
7. OK. The student has paraphrased without using language or structure from the source and has cited the source with a footnote.
8. Plagiarized. The student has used words from the source without quotation marks (*combined the two strands, lethal cocktail*) and has not cited the source in a footnote.
9. OK. The student has placed exact words from the source in quotation marks and has paraphrased other ideas from the source and documented the source with a footnote.
10. Plagiarized. The student has used the structure of the source and has simply plugged in synonyms for the words of the source (*beginnings* for *origins, the concentration camps* for *Auschwitz, seen* for *traced, momentous combination* for *fateful coupling*).

EXERCISE 63-4 Avoiding plagiarism in *Chicago* papers, page 99

1. OK. In addition to documenting the source with a footnote, the student has enclosed exact words from the source in quotation marks.

2. Plagiarized. Although the student has documented the source with a footnote, the student has used language from the source without enclosing it in quotation marks.

3. Plagiarized. The student has copied much of the sentence word-for-word from the source without using quotation marks.

4. OK. In addition to documenting the source with a footnote, the student has paraphrased it without borrowing its language or structure.

5. Plagiarized. Although the sentence ends with a note, the student has paraphrased the original source far too closely, borrowing structure from the original and plugging in synonyms (*failed to fire* for *jammed*, *pliant* for *soft*, *bent out of shape* for *deformed*, and so on).

6. OK. In addition to documenting the source, the student has paraphrased it without borrowing its language or structure.

7. Plagiarized. Although the sentence ends with a note, the student has copied a long phrase from the source word-for-word without using quotation marks (*Custer's troops used ammunition belts made from scrap leather*).

8. OK. In addition to documenting the source, the student has paraphrased it without borrowing its language or structure.

9. Plagiarized. After the introductory clause, the student has copied the source word-for-word without using quotation marks and has failed to provide a footnote to document the source.

10. OK. In addition to documenting the source with a footnote, the student has placed borrowed language in quotation marks and has used brackets around words that do not appear in the original source.

EXERCISE 63-5 Avoiding plagiarism in *Chicago* papers, page 101

1. OK. The student has paraphrased without using language or structure from the source.

2. Plagiarized. The student has borrowed phrases (*depended on its dogs*, *from the beginning*) from the source without enclosing them in quotation marks.

3. Plagiarized. The student has borrowed words from the source and rearranged them but has not indicated the borrowing with quotation marks.

4. OK. The student has enclosed exact language from the source in quotation marks.

5. Plagiarized. The writer's paraphrase uses the structure of the source's sentence while simply substituting synonyms for most words (*canine* for *dog*, *haul* for *pull*, *taken secretly* for *kidnapped*).

EXERCISE 63-6 Avoiding plagiarism in *Chicago* papers, page 102

1. Plagiarized. The student has used the exact language of the source (*had killed him with poisoned mushrooms*) without enclosing the words in quotation marks. In addition, the phrase *most likely but not quite certain* is too close to the language of the source to be an acceptable paraphrase.

2. OK. The student has paraphrased ideas from the source without borrowing language or sentence structure.

3. OK. The student has used quotation marks to enclose exact words from the source.

4. Plagiarized. The student has paraphrased the source too closely, using the sentence structure of the source and substituting synonyms for the language of the source (*prepared the way* for *cleared the ground*, *needed only to bide her time* for *only had to wait*).

5. OK. The student has paraphrased ideas without borrowing language or structure from the source.

EXERCISE 63-7 Recognizing common knowledge in *Chicago* papers, page 103

1. Common knowledge. This was a widely covered occurrence in modern history that continues to make news. It needs no citation.

2. Needs citation. This information is likely to be found only in a narrow range of sources; it may not be known even to some well-informed students of history. The source should be cited.

3. Common knowledge. Information about the life and death of a well-known figure is often common knowledge. The circumstances of Lincoln's assassination in particular have been exhaustively reported.

4. Needs citation. This is specific information about a subject unfamiliar to many readers, so the source should be cited.

5. Needs citation. The eruption of the volcano on Krakatau might be considered common knowledge, but specific information about the effects of the eruption should be cited.

6. Common knowledge. This general information about the Vietnam era appears in many sources, so no citation is required.

7. Common knowledge. This information would appear in any source about the Hillary expedition, which is credited as the first successful ascent of Everest. A well-known fact about a famous event needs no citation.

8. Common knowledge. This is a widely publicized fact about the life of the well-known general. Widely publicized information about famous figures in history generally needs no citation.

9. Common knowledge. This kind of general information about the underground railroad does not need to be cited.

10. Needs citation. This information is likely to come from a narrow range of sources. Because of the specificity of this statement, the writer should cite the source.

EXERCISE 63-8 Integrating sources in *Chicago* papers, page 105

1. OK. The student uses a signal phrase and places the exact words of the source in quotation marks.

2. This sentence is unacceptable. The student has put words in quotation marks that are slightly different from the words in the source. The following is an acceptable revision:
   According to Barbara Hanawalt, "Practices associated with normal births in medieval Europe are shrouded in secrecy."[2]

3. The second sentence is a dropped quotation. The student has failed to provide a signal phrase naming the author. The following is an acceptable revision:
   "Practices associated with normal births in medieval Europe are shrouded in secrecy," Barbara Hanawalt notes, "not because the births were hidden at the time, but because they were a woman's ritual and women did not pass on information about them in writing."[3]

4. OK. The student has smoothly integrated quoted words from the source into the sentence. The student also has introduced the quotation with a signal phrase and enclosed it in quotation marks.

5. OK. The student has enclosed exact words from the source in quotation marks and has used an ellipsis mark to show where words have been omitted.

6. The passage is unacceptable. The student has correctly indented the long quotation from the source but should not have used quotation marks around the indented quotation. In addition, an indented quotation should be introduced by a complete sentence, usually followed by a colon. The following is an acceptable revision:

Barbara Hanawalt notes that little information has come down to us about normal births in the Middle Ages:

> Practices associated with normal births in medieval Europe are shrouded in secrecy, not because the births were hidden at the time, but because they were a woman's ritual and women did not pass on information about them in writing. Indeed, we can be quite sure that the event of a birth was well known within the immediate community. Living close together, the neighbors would hear the cries of a woman in labor and would observe the midwife and female friends gathering around. But what occurred in the birthing chamber was not known to the men listening outside, and so it was not recorded.[6]

7. This passage is unacceptable. The student has omitted material between the two sentences that appear in quotation marks and has failed to indicate the omission with an ellipsis mark. The following is an acceptable revision:

> Little is known today about normal births in the Middle Ages. Barbara Hanawalt explains that births "were a woman's ritual and women did not pass on information about them in writing. . . . But what occurred in the birthing chamber was not known to the men listening outside, and so it was not recorded."[7]

8. OK. The student has enclosed exact words from the source in quotation marks and has used brackets to indicate an addition that clarifies the quoted material.

9. The material in quotation marks is a dropped quotation. The student has enclosed the words of the source in quotation marks but has not used a signal phrase identifying the author and has not provided enough context for the quotation. The following is an acceptable revision:

> Only abnormal births are described in learned medieval writings. Barbara Hanawalt explains why: "Male doctors never attended a normal birth, so they knew nothing about them. They were called in only when surgery was needed."[9]

10. OK. The student has smoothly integrated the quotation into the sentence and has introduced it with a signal phrase.

EXERCISE 63-9 Integrating sources in *Chicago* papers, page 107

1. This sentence is unacceptable. The words in quotation marks differ slightly from those in the source. Words in quotation marks must follow the source exactly (unless brackets or an ellipsis mark indicates a change). The following is an acceptable revision:

> According to Jeffrey Goldberg, Hezbollah "quickly became the most successful terrorist organization in modern history."[1]

2. This sentence is unacceptable. The student has failed to put quotation marks around some words taken directly from the source (*Hezbollah, with bases in the Bekaa and in Beirut's southern suburbs*). The following is an acceptable revision:

> According to Jeffrey Goldberg, "Hezbollah, with bases in the Bekaa and in Beirut's southern suburbs, quickly became the most successful terrorist organization in modern history."[2]

3. OK. The student has introduced the quotation with a signal phrase and has enclosed exact words from the source in quotation marks.

4. The second sentence is a dropped quotation. The student has failed to provide a signal phrase naming the author. The following is an acceptable revision:

> Hezbollah has been successful. As Jeffrey Goldberg points out, "It has served as a role model for terror groups around the world."[4]

5. OK. The student has introduced the quotation with a signal phrase and has placed exact words from the source in quotation marks.

6. OK. The student has used an ellipsis mark to show where words from the source have been omitted, and otherwise the quotation is word-for-word accurate.

7. This passage is unacceptable. The student should not have used quotation marks around an indented quotation and should have introduced the long quotation with a complete sentence ending in a colon. (The student has correctly used brackets and an ellipsis mark to indicate changes in the source.) The following is an acceptable revision:

> Jeffrey Goldberg explains the terrifying precision of a Hezbollah attack:
>
> > [Hezbollah] virtually invented the multipronged terror attack when . . . it synchronized the suicide bombings, in Beirut, of the United States Marine barracks and an apartment building housing a contingent of French peacekeepers. Those attacks occurred just twenty seconds apart; a third part of the plan, to destroy the compound of the Italian peacekeeping contingent, is said to have been jettisoned when the planners learned that the Italians were sleeping in tents, not in a high-rise building.[7]

8. OK. The student has enclosed language from the source in quotation marks and has used brackets to indicate that a word from the source has been changed (from *invented* to *inventing*) to fit the grammar of the sentence.

9. This sentence is unacceptable. The words in quotation marks differ from those in the source. Words in quotation marks must follow the source exactly (unless changes have been indicated with brackets or an ellipsis mark). The following is an acceptable revision:

> Hezbollah scrapped a plan to bomb a third location in Beirut in 1983, explains Jeffrey Goldberg, "when the planners learned that the [intended victims] were . . . not in a high-rise building."[9]

10. OK. The student has used brackets to enclose explanatory words added to the quotation, and the quotation is otherwise word-for-word accurate.

EXERCISE 63-10 Integrating sources in *Chicago* papers, page 109

1. OK. The student has enclosed words from the source in quotation marks and has named the author in a signal phrase.

2. This sentence contains a dropped quotation. The student has failed to provide a signal phrase naming the author. The following is an acceptable revision:

> In the Anglo-French wars prior to 1815, historian Kennedy points out, "victory . . . went to the Power—or better, since both Britain and France usually had allies, to the Great Power coalition—with the greater capacity to maintain credit and to keep on raising supplies."[2]

3. This sentence is unacceptable. The student has left out words from the source (*would look to a more powerful ally for loans and reinforcements in order to*) but has not indicated the omission with an ellipsis mark. In addition, the student has added the word *could*, which is not in the source, without putting brackets around it. The following is an acceptable revision:

> Kennedy notes that in the wars between Britain and France before 1815, the key to victory was building a coalition of countries so that "a belligerent whose resources were fading . . . [could] keep itself in the fight."[3]

4. OK. The student has quoted the source correctly and has enclosed borrowed words in quotation marks.
5. OK. The student has put the exact words of the source in quotation marks and has used ellipsis marks to indicate omissions from the source. The student also has used brackets to enclose a word that makes the quotation fit within the grammar of the sentence.

EXERCISE 63-11 Integrating sources in *Chicago* papers, page 110

1. This sentence contains a dropped quotation. The student has failed to provide a signal phrase naming the author. The following is an acceptable revision:

    Sampson quotes the Mandelas' daughter as saying that after Mandela and his wife, Winnie, separated, "It was as if they did not exist for each other."[1]
2. OK. The student has enclosed exact words from the source in quotation marks and has named the author in a signal phrase.
3. This sentence is unacceptable. The quotation is not word-for-word accurate from the source: The student has omitted a colon but has not indicated the omission with an ellipsis mark, and has added the word *and* but has not enclosed it in brackets. The following is an acceptable revision:

    Sampson explains that when Winnie Mandela served as deputy minister of arts, "she became openly disloyal . . . [and] accused the ANC of being preoccupied with appeasing whites."[3]
4. OK. The student has enclosed words from the source in quotation marks and has used brackets around material added to explain the quotation.
5. OK. The student has enclosed exact words from the source in quotation marks and has named the author in a signal phrase.

EXERCISE 63-12 *Chicago* documentation: identifying elements of sources, page 111

1. a. In *Chicago* style for a work with three authors, all authors' names are given in full.
2. a. *Chicago* style uses the abbreviation "no.," not a period, before the issue number.
3. b. The *Chicago* bibliography entry should include the title of the entire work as well as the number and title of the volume.
4. a. The volume and issue numbers are given. Only the first page of the article is given in the database listing, so the page number is followed by a plus sign in the bibliography entry.
5. a. The database record does not give a DOI, but it does give a document number at the end of the article, so in *Chicago* style the document number should be included in the bibliography entry.
6. b. The name of the author of the work appears first, and the words "Translated by" are spelled out following the title.
7. a. The name of the reviewer should appear first, followed by the title of the review, the words "Review of," and then the title of the work reviewed and the author of the work.
8. a. In *Chicago* style for a magazine, the date should be given in month-day-year order with the month spelled out.
9. a. The position of the Library of Congress at the top of the page and at the bottom left indicates that it is the sponsor.
10. b. The Web site title and the sponsor of the site are given after the title of the document.

EXERCISE 63-13 *Chicago* documentation: notes, page 117

1. a. In a *Chicago* note, the names of all authors appear in normal order, first name first.

2. b. When a source has been previously cited, the note should appear in shortened form. Only the last name of the author, a short form of the title (in this case the whole title because it is only four words), and a page number are required.
3. a. For two consecutive notes from the same source, *Chicago* recommends using the abbreviation "Ibid." and the page number in the second note.
4. a. In a *Chicago* note, commas (not periods) are used after the author's name and after the title of the article.
5. b. The exact date of a weekly magazine must be given in the note.
6. b. A short form of the title (in this case the full title because it is only two words) should be set off with commas, not with parentheses, and the author's last name, not first and last, should be used.
7. a. For a work with two authors, both authors' names must be given; "and others" is used only when a work has four or more authors.
8. b. The note begins with the name of the person interviewed.
9. a. The note includes the URL for the article.
10. b. The note for an online article includes the volume and issue numbers if available.

EXERCISE 63-14 *Chicago* documentation: notes, page 119

1. b. In a *Chicago* note, the name of the author appears in normal order, first name first.
2. a. When a source has been previously cited, only the last name of the author, a short form of the title, and a page number are required.
3. a. Both authors' last names are given, even in a shortened note.
4. a. Commas, not periods, separate the elements in a *Chicago* note.
5. b. A work with an unknown author is cited by its title.
6. b. The title of the full Web site is included after the title of the short document.
7. a. A note for a magazine article includes only the date, not the volume and issue numbers.
8. b. In a *Chicago* note for a newspaper article, the section letter or number, not the page number, is cited.
9. b. For two consecutive notes from the same page in the same source, *Chicago* recommends using only the abbreviation "Ibid." in the second note.
10. b. The note includes the sponsor of the site, National Public Radio, as well as the title of the site (NPR).

EXERCISE 63-15 *Chicago* documentation: notes, page 123

1. b. In a *Chicago* note, the names of all authors are given first name first.
2. b. In *Chicago* note style, all months of the year are spelled out in full.
3. b. In *Chicago* style, all dates are given in month-day-year order.
4. a. In *Chicago* style, the word "in" comes after the title of the short work and before the title of the collection.
5. a. *Chicago* note style does not use angle brackets around URLs.
6. b. In a *Chicago* note, the title of the online magazine precedes the date of posting.
7. a. In *Chicago* style, a note for a work without an author begins with the title of the work.
8. a. A note for a review includes only the title and author, not complete publishing information, for the work reviewed.
9. b. A note for a source cited earlier in the paper gives the author's last name and a short title of the source.

10. b. For a source cited in the immediately preceding note, the word "Ibid." is used in place of the author and short title. The page number is given if it is different from the number in the preceding note.

EXERCISE 63-16 *Chicago* documentation: bibliography, page 127

1. b. In a *Chicago* bibliography entry, the author's name is given last name first.
2. a. In a *Chicago* bibliography entry, all authors' names are given for works with two or more authors.
3. b. In a *Chicago* bibliography entry for a journal article, the year in parentheses follows the volume and issue numbers.
4. a. Only the date and page numbers are given for a magazine article in a *Chicago* bibliography.
5. a. In *Chicago* bibliography style, the term "edited by" is spelled out in full before the editor's name.
6. b. The word "unpublished" is not used in a *Chicago* bibliography entry. The quotation marks indicate that the dissertation is unpublished.
7. b. In a *Chicago* bibliography entry, the sponsor of the Web site is given in addition to the title of the site.
8. a. For an article accessed through a database, *Chicago* requires a persistent or stable URL if one is listed.
9. b. A *Chicago* bibliography entry for an online article includes the name and date of the publication, as for a print article.
10. b. Because the student has used dialogue from the film and has not emphasized one person's contribution, the bibliography entry begins with the title of the film, not the director's name.

EXERCISE 63-17 *Chicago* documentation: bibliography, page 131

1. b. A *Chicago* bibliography entry for a newspaper article gives the section letter, not the page number.
2. a. In a *Chicago* bibliography entry for an essay appearing in an anthology, the author of the essay is listed first, followed by the essay title, the anthology title, and the editor of the anthology.
3. b. A *Chicago* bibliography entry for a book review lists the name of the reviewer first and the name of the book's author after the title of the book.
4. b. A *Chicago* bibliography entry for a journal citation includes the year as well as the volume and issue number.
5. a. In a *Chicago* bibliography entry for a letter in a collection, the date of the letter is inverted (in day-month-year form).
6. a. For a work from a Web site in a *Chicago* bibliography, the date of access is included if the source itself has no date.
7. b. Information about a discussion list posting is included only in a note, not in the bibliography.
8. b. A *Chicago* bibliography entry for a book does not include page numbers. Page numbers are included in a note.
9. a. A *Chicago* bibliography entry for a movie includes the format the student viewed (DVD).
10. a. If there is no DOI, a *Chicago* bibliography entry for an article found in a database includes the name of the database and the document number.

EXERCISE 63-18 *Chicago* documentation: bibliography, page 135

1. a. In *Chicago* bibliography entries, the first author's name is reversed, but subsequent names are listed in normal order.
2. b. In a *Chicago* bibliography entry for a Web site with no named author, the entry begins with the title.
3. a. When two sources in a *Chicago* bibliography are by the same author, the sources are listed alphabetically by title.
4. b. E-mail messages are treated like personal communications and are not included in the bibliography.
5. b. In a *Chicago* bibliography entry for a film on DVD, the original release date of the film, if known, is listed before the DVD distribution information.
6. a. In a *Chicago* bibliography entry for a source quoted in another source, the publication information for the original source is required.
7. a. A *Chicago* bibliography entry for an article accessed through an online database includes both print publication information and the URL for the database.
8. a. In *Chicago* bibliography entries for journal articles, the volume and issue numbers are included along with the year.
9. b. In a *Chicago* bibliography entry for a newspaper article, the section letter, if available, is sufficient; a page number is not included.
10. a. In a *Chicago* bibliography entry for a work with three or more authors, all authors' names are listed.

EXERCISE 63-19 *Chicago* documentation, page 138

1. True. Notes are required for summaries and paraphrases as well as for quotations.
2. False. The bibliography may include both the works cited in the notes and works the writer consulted but did not cite.
3. False. A note is needed for each reference to a source; abbreviated notes are used for subsequent references to a source.
4. False. For two consecutive notes from the same source, *Chicago* recommends using the abbreviation "Ibid." and the page number in the second note.
5. True. The bibliography is organized alphabetically so that readers can quickly find the source cited in the paper.
6. False. *Chicago* style does not require angle brackets around a URL.
7. True. The note format and the bibliography format differ slightly.
8. False. Notes begin with a paragraph-style indent, but in the bibliography each entry begins against the left margin, and any additional lines are indented.
9. True. Either footnotes or endnotes are acceptable.
10. False. Note numbers in the text of the paper appear in superscript (they are slightly raised above the line of text). The numbers are not enclosed in parentheses.

Acknowledgments

Title page from *The American Historical Review*, Volume 108, Number 2 (April 2003). Copyright © 2003. Reprinted with the permission of Oxford University Press.

John R. Anderson, title and copyright pages from *Cognitive Psychology and Its Implications*, Sixth Edition. Copyright © 2005, 2000, 1995, 1990, 1985, 1980 by Worth Publishers and W. H. Freeman and Company. Reprinted with the permission of Worth Publishers, Inc.

Jean Baudrillard, excerpt from "The Ideological Genesis of Needs," translated by Charles Levin, from *For a Critique of the Political Economy of the Sign*. Copyright © 1969 by Jean Baudrillard. Reprinted with the permission of Telos Press Publishing.

Martin Bernal, *Black Athena: The Afroasiatic Roots of Classical Civilization*, Volume I: *The Fabrication of Ancient Greece 1785–1985*. Copyright © 1987 by Martin Bernal. Reprinted with the permission of Rutgers University Press.

Bruce Bower, "Good grief: Bereaved adjust well without airing emotion," *Science News* (March 2, 2002): 131–132; and "Men of prey," *Science News* (July 27, 2002): 59–60. Reprinted with permission of Science News.

Courtesy of Brookings Institution's Brown Center on Education Policy and author Tom Loveless. Photo by © Jim Young/Reuters.

Jared Diamond, "Twilight at Easter" [Review of the books *The Enigmas of Easter Island*, by J. Flenly & P. Bahn, and *Among Stone Giants: The Life of Katherine Routledge and Her Remarkable Expedition to Easter Island*, by J. A. Van Tilburg]. *New York Review of Books*, 51(5), 6, 8–10. Copyright © 2004 by Jared Diamond. Reprinted with permission from The New York Review of Books.

Ophira Edut (ed.), title page from *Body Outlaws: Rewriting the Rules of Beauty and Body Image*. Copyright © 2004 by Ophira Edut, Rebecca Walker. Reprinted with the permission of Seal Press, a member of the Perseus Group.

Screen shots from Gale Expanded Academic ASAP Infotrac. Copyright © 2013, a part of Cengage Learning, Inc. Reproduced by permission. www.cengage.com/permissions.

From Frederic Golden, "Electric Wind." *Los Angeles Times* 24 Dec. 1990: B1. Reprinted by permission of the author.

Marguerite Holloway, excerpt from "When Medicine Meets Literature" from *Scientific American* 292, no. 5 (May 2005). Reproduced with permission. Copyright © 2005 by Scientific American, a division of Nature America, Inc. All rights reserved. This page includes an image by Flynn Larsen, copyright © Flynn Larsen, reprinted by permission.

Naomi Lamoreaux, Daniel M. G. Raff, and Peter Temin, excerpt from "Beyond Markets and Hierarchies: Toward a New Synthesis of American Business History" from *The American Historical Review*, Volume 108, Number 2 (April 2003). Copyright © 2003. Reprinted with the permission of Oxford University Press.

Niccolò Machiavelli, title page from *Florentine Histories*, translated by Laura F. Banfield and Harvey C. Mansfield Jr. Copyright © 1988 by Princeton University Press. Reprinted with the permission of Princeton University Press.

Michael Scammell, "The Russian Nobility under the Red Terror," from *The New York Review of Books*. Copyright © 2013 NYREV Inc. Photo: Douglas Smith, reproduced by permission.

From James W. Pennebaker, *The Secret Life of Pronouns: What Our Words Say about Us*, Bloomsbury Press, 2011. Reprinted by permission.

Juliet B. Schor and Douglas B. Holt (eds.), *The Consumer Society Reader*. Copyright © 2000. Reprinted with the permission of The New Press.

Scientific American, table of contents page from *Scientific American* 292, no. 5 (May 2005): 6. Reproduced with permission. Copyright © 2005 by Scientific American, a division of Nature America, Inc. All rights reserved. This page includes images by Matt Collins, copyright © Matt Collins, reprinted by permission, and an image by Flynn Larsen, copyright © Flynn Larsen, reprinted by permission.

Screen shots of *Shakespeare's World at Emory University*, http://shakespeare.emory.edu/. Courtesy of Harry Rusche and Emory University.

Robert Skidelsky. "Family Values," *New York Review of Books*, December 16, 1999, pp. 24–29. Copyright © 1999 by Robert Skidelsky. Reprinted with permission from The New York Review of Books.

From *Slate*, March 22, 2011. Copyright © The Slate Group. All rights reserved. Used by permission and protected by the Copyright Laws of the United States. The printing, copying, redistribution, or retransmission of this Content without express written permission is prohibited.

Courtesy of *Southern Cultures* and the University of North Carolina Press, and Project MUSE, The Johns Hopkins University Press.